Simple Desserts

MADE SPECIAL WITH

Cool Whip®

PUBLICATIONS INTERNATIONAL, LTD.

This edition published by Publications International, Ltd., 7373 N. Cicero Ave.,
Lincolnwood, IL 60646.

ANGEL FLAKE, BAKER'S, BIRDS EYE, COOL WHIP, COOL WHIP LITE, ENTENMANN'S,
GERMAN'S, JELL-O, KOOL-AID, KRAFT and PHILADELPHIA BRAND are registered
trademarks of Kraft General Foods, Inc., Glenview, IL 60025.

Product Group:	Dan Marchetti, Michele Buck
Project Coordinator:	Trisha Clark
Project Advisors:	Marie Joseph, Theresa Kreinen
Recipe Development and Food Styling:	Cathy Garvey, Leslie Medina-Scocca, Catherine Paukner, Roberta Rall. **Assistants:** Freida Grob and Erna Krueger
Photography:	Allan Newman and Eugene Knowles Newman O'Neill Group, Inc., New York
Prop Stylist:	Heather Bean
Illustrations:	Rowena J. Vargas

Pictured on the front cover (*clockwise from top left*): Black Forest Torte (*page 31*),
Wild Side Sundaes (*page 94*), Frozen Strawberry-Yogurt Pie (*page 67*), Lemon Cheese
Square (*page 62*).

Pictured on the back cover (*clockwise from top left*): Easter Bonnet Cake (*page 36*)
and Cannoli Parfaits (*page 36*); Crazy Colored Halloween Desserts (*page 75*) and Boo
the Ghost (*page 72*); Candy Cane Cake (*page 16*), Chocolate Peppermint Pie (*page 16*)
and Merry Berry Dessert (*page 17*); Stars and Stripes Dessert (*page 53*).

ISBN: 0-7853-0589-0

Manufactured in U.S.A.

8 7 6 5 4 3 2 1

Simple Desserts
MADE SPECIAL WITH
Cool Whip®

Introduction · 4
COOL WHIP Basics, Crust Basics, Toasting Nuts, Tips for Success, Coconut Know-How, Baking Chocolate Know-How, Easy Chocolate Garnishes, Easy Fruit Garnishes, Gumdrop Garnishes

'Tis the Season · 14
Christmas, New Year's, The Diet Resolution, Super Bowl Sunday, Curing the Winter Blues, Valentine's Day, President's Day, St. Patrick's Day

Spring Sensations · 34
Brunch, Easter, Mother's Day, Baby Shower, Berry Season

Summertime Celebrations · 50
Red, White and Blue Holidays, Father's Day, Weddings and Anniversaries, Graduation, Family Reunions, Summertime Pies

Autumn Delights · 68
Apple Harvest, Back to School, Halloween, Fall Get-Togethers, Thanksgiving

Year-Round Fun for Kids · 82
Cookies and More, The Circus Comes to Town, Little League, Birthday Party, Playing in the Backyard

Index · 95

Introduction

Special desserts that are fun and easy to make add a festive touch to any celebration. COOL WHIP Whipped Topping is that special ingredient that helps make every occasion an extraordinary one. Whatever the event or day, these fabulous recipes will help make each one a memorable occasion for family and friends.

Included is a whole calendar of recipes that will help you entertain with style and ease throughout the year. For quick and easy reference, this book is divided by seasons. Recipes for the winter holidays and events can be found in the chapter "'Tis the Season." If you're looking for a special dessert to make for Christmas, Valentine's Day or even St. Patrick's Day, this is where to look.

"Spring Sensations" will provide you with dessert ideas for Easter, Mother's Day, Sunday brunch and baby showers. Another chapter includes favorite summer celebrations such as graduations, picnics and family reunions. "Autumn Delights" features desserts that make fall festivities special. Last but not least, an entire chapter is devoted to kids' favorites—perfect activities for year-round fun.

Simple Desserts Made Special with COOL WHIP is more than a collection of wonderful recipes—it's also a guide to creative entertaining. The easy-to-follow instructions are the key to the delicious desserts presented on the following pages. You'll find everything you need to know in order to duplicate the recipes in your own kitchen. Every recipe takes less than 30 minutes to prepare (excluding refrigerating and freezing time) so there's more time for you to spend with your family and guests.

COOL WHIP Basics

How To Thaw COOL WHIP

- Place tub of COOL WHIP Whipped Topping, unopened, in the refrigerator. For complete thawing, allow these times:
  - 1 hour for 4-ounce tub
  - 4 hours for 8-ounce tub
  - 5 hours for 12-ounce tub
  - 6 hours for 16-ounce tub

- Thawing COOL WHIP in the microwave is not recommended. The timing is too critical. A second or so too long in the microwave will liquify COOL WHIP.

How To Store COOL WHIP

- For long-term storage, keep COOL WHIP Whipped Topping in the freezer. Once thawed, keep refrigerated no more than 2 weeks. For longer storage, refreeze. Don't let the container stand in a hot kitchen—the topping will soften and may begin to liquify.

■ ■ ■

COOL WHIP Whipped Topping comes in four different sizes. To estimate your recipe needs, the content amounts are listed in the chart below.

	COOL WHIP Non-Dairy	COOL WHIP Extra Creamy	COOL WHIP LITE	COOL WHIP Chocolate
Tub Size	**Amount**	**Amount**	**Amount**	**Amount**
4 ounces	1³/₄ cups			
8 ounces	3¹/₂ cups	3 cups	3¹/₄ cups	3 cups
12 ounces	5¹/₄ cups	4¹/₂ cups	5 cups	
16 ounces	7 cups			

COOL WHIP Whipped Toppings

Serving Tips for COOL WHIP

- COOL WHIP Whipped Topping is best thawed before use, but it can also be used as a topping before it has thawed entirely. Take it right from freezer or refrigerator and spoon onto dessert about 5 minutes before serving.

- Thaw COOL WHIP Whipped Topping completely before measuring or stirring into ingredients.

- When serving thawed frozen fruit with COOL WHIP Whipped Topping, drain the fruit first. The juice may make the topping appear curdled.

- Stir a few drops of food coloring into thawed COOL WHIP Whipped Topping to make tinted frostings and toppings.

- For fluted borders and rosettes, spoon thawed COOL WHIP Whipped Topping into a pastry bag or decorating tube and press through desired tip.

- When using COOL WHIP Whipped Topping as a frosting or as an ingredient in a frosting, store cake in refrigerator.

How To Use COOL WHIP in Recipes

- COOL WHIP Non-Dairy, Extra Creamy and COOL WHIP LITE Whipped Toppings can usually be used interchangeably in recipes. If COOL WHIP LITE is used with gelatin or higher acid fruits, the recipe may not set as firmly. Make sure to use the cup measurement specified in the recipe.

- Substitute equal amounts of COOL WHIP Whipped Topping for sweetened whipped cream. When a recipe calls for liquid cream that is to be whipped, double the measure and substitute COOL WHIP.

- All recipes prepared with COOL WHIP Whipped Topping should be stored either in the refrigerator or the freezer.

Easy Garnishes with COOL WHIP

Whipped Topping Dollops

1. Swirl spoon, held upright, through thawed COOL WHIP, creating rippled surface on the whipped topping.

2. Dip spoon into rippled whipped topping to scoop up heaping spoonful of whipped topping, maintaining rippled surface.

3. Gently touch spoon onto surface of dessert and release whipped topping gradually onto surface, pulling spoon up into a crowning tip.

Whipped Topping Piping

Insert decorating tip into pastry bag; fill with thawed COOL WHIP Whipped Topping. Fold down pastry bag. Holding bag firmly with one hand and squeezing topping down into tip, guide tip around surface to be decorated. If desired, double back whipped topping at intervals for decorative wave effect.

Crust Basics

The simplest approach is to purchase a 9-inch ready-to-use crumb crust. These are available in 6-ounce packages and in a variety of flavors. However, you can make your own. Here's how:

Use packaged graham cracker crumbs or follow one of the following methods for crushing crackers or cookies:

Plastic Bag Method: Place crackers or cookies in large zipper-style plastic bag. Press out excess air; seal. Using a rolling pin, roll the crackers until they are crushed into fine crumbs.

Food Processor Method: Break crackers or cookies. Place in food processor container; cover. Process until fine crumbs form.

To Prepare Crust: Mix 1 1/2 cups graham cracker or cookie crumbs, 3 tablespoons sugar and 1/3 cup margarine, melted. Press onto bottom and up sides of 9-inch pie plate. Refrigerate until ready to use.

To Toast Nuts

Heat oven to 400°F. Spread nuts in an even layer in a shallow baking pan. Toast 8 to 10 minutes or until golden brown, stirring frequently.

Tips for Success

Some Tips for Success When Using JELL-O Brand Gelatin

- To make a mixture that is clear and uniformly set, be sure the gelatin is *completely* dissolved in boiling water or other boiling liquid before adding the cold liquid.

- To store prepared gelatin overnight or longer, cover to prevent drying.

- Always store gelatin cakes, desserts or pies in the refrigerator.

Some Tips for Success When Using JELL-O Instant Pudding and Pie Filling

- Always use *cold* milk. Beat pudding mix slowly, not vigorously.

- For best results, use whole or 2% lowfat milk. Skim milk, reconstituted nonfat dry milk, light cream or half-and-half can also be used.

- Always store prepared pudding desserts, snacks and pies in the refrigerator.

Coconut Know-How

- **To Store Coconut:** Unopened packages of BAKER'S ANGEL FLAKE Coconut can be kept on your kitchen shelf. After opening the package, store the coconut in a tightly closed package or in an airtight container. Refrigerate or freeze coconut for up to 6 months.

- **To Toast Coconut:** Heat oven to 350°F. Spread 1 1/3 cups BAKER'S ANGEL FLAKE Coconut in an even layer in a shallow baking pan. Toast 7 to 12 minutes or until lightly browned, stirring the coconut frequently so that it will brown evenly. Or, toast in microwave in a microwavable bowl on HIGH 5 minutes, stirring several times.

- **To Tint Coconut:** Place 1 cup BAKER'S ANGEL FLAKE Coconut in a plastic bag. Dilute a few drops of food coloring with 1/2 teaspoon of water and add to the coconut. Close the bag and shake until the coconut is evenly tinted. Repeat with more food coloring and water for a darker shade, if desired.

Baking Chocolate Know-How

- Store chocolate in a cool, dry place, below 75°F, if possible, but not in the refrigerator.

- We strongly recommend that you use the microwave method for melting chocolate. Chocolate scorches easily on the top of the stove so use very low heat and a heavy saucepan when using this method.

- Use the type of chocolate called for in a recipe. As a rule, semi-sweet chocolate and unsweetened chocolate are not interchangeable in recipes.

How to Melt Chocolate

- **Microwave Method:** Heat 1 unwrapped square of BAKER'S Semi-Sweet or Unsweetened Chocolate or 1 unwrapped 4-ounce bar of BAKER'S GERMAN'S Sweet Chocolate, broken in half, in microwavable bowl on HIGH 1 to 2 minutes or until almost melted, stirring halfway through heating time. Semi-Sweet and GERMAN'S Sweet Chocolates will retain some of their original shapes. Remove from oven. **Stir until chocolate is completely melted.** Add 10 seconds for each additional square of Semi-Sweet or Unsweetened Chocolate.

- **Top of Stove Method:** Place unwrapped chocolate in heavy saucepan on very low heat; stir constantly until just melted.

Easy Chocolate Garnishes

Chocolate Curls

1. Melt 4 squares BAKER'S Semi-Sweet Chocolate. Spread with spatula into very thin layer on cookie sheet. Refrigerate about 10 minutes or until firm, but still pliable.

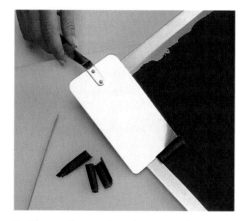

2. To make curls, slip tip of straight-side metal spatula under chocolate. Push spatula firmly along cookie sheet, under chocolate, so chocolate curls as it is pushed. (If chocolate is too firm to curl, let stand a few minutes at room temperature; refrigerate again if it becomes too soft.)

3. Carefully pick up each chocolate curl by inserting toothpick in center. Lift onto wax paper-lined cookie sheet.

4. Refrigerate about 15 minutes or until firm. Arrange on desserts. (Lift with toothpick to prevent breakage or melting.) Refrigerate until ready to serve.

Dipping Fruit and Nuts

Melt BAKER'S Semi-Sweet Chocolate or BAKER'S GERMAN'S Sweet Chocolate. Dip fruit or nuts into chocolate, covering at least half; let excess chocolate drip off. Let stand or refrigerate on wax paper-lined tray about 30 minutes or until chocolate is firm.

Chocolate Cutouts

1. Melt 4 squares BAKER'S Semi-Sweet Chocolate. Pour onto wax paper-lined cookie sheet; spread to ⅛-inch thickness with spatula. Refrigerate about 15 minutes or until firm.

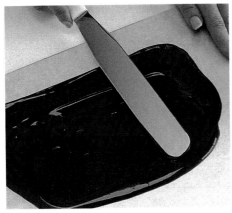

2. Cut out shapes with cookie cutters.

3. Immediately lift shapes carefully from wax paper with spatula or knife. Refrigerate until ready to use.

Chocolate Drizzle

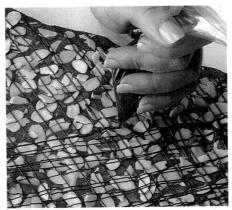

1. Place 1 square BAKER'S Semi-Sweet Chocolate in zipper-style plastic sandwich bag. Close bag tightly. Microwave on HIGH about 1 minute or until chocolate is melted. Fold down top of bag tightly; snip tiny piece off corner (about ⅛ inch).

2. Holding top of bag tightly, drizzle chocolate through opening over brownies, cookies, cakes or desserts.

Easy Fruit Garnishes

Citrus Twists

1. With sharp knife, cut orange, lemon or lime into thin slices.

2. Cut slit through slices to centers.

3. Twist slices from slits in opposite directions to form twists.

Fruit Fans

1. With sharp knife, cut drained canned pear halves into thin slices (about 5 or 6), cutting up to, but not through, stem ends. (Use same technique for strawberries.)

2. Hold stem end in place and gently fan out slices from stem before placing on plate for fruit desserts or using as garnish.

Gumdrop Garnishes

Gumdrop Shapes

1. Flatten gumdrops with rolling pin on a smooth flat surface or sheet of wax paper sprinkled with sugar. Roll until very thin (about $1/16$-inch thick), turning frequently to coat with sugar. Cut into desired shapes.

2. For **Gumdrop Flowers**, hold flattened gumdrop at center; overlap edges slightly to give petal effect, pressing piece together at base to resemble flower. For open blossom, bend gumdrop petals outward from center. Insert small piece of gumdrop in centers with toothpick, if desired. Use toothpick to attach flowers to cake if necessary.

Gumdrop Ribbon

1. Line up gumdrops in a row on a smooth flat surface or a sheet of wax paper sprinkled with sugar. Flatten into long strips with a rolling pin, turning frequently to coat with sugar.

2. Cut flattened gumdrops into a strip as needed.

Note: If you can't find large gumdrops, simply press several small gumdrops together before flattening with the rolling pin. Chewy fruit snack rolls can also be used for cutting out shapes.

'Tis the Season

This most wonderful time of the year provides a variety of holidays and other events to celebrate with family and friends.

Create your own delicious Yuletide traditions with a mouth-watering selection of holiday recipes such as **Chocolate Peppermint Pie, Candy Cane Cake** or **Christmas Ornament Desserts.**

After the holidays, our collection of lower calorie treats will help you keep an eye on your waistline. You won't believe **Chocolate Mousse** allows you to stick to your diet resolution.

Fan or not, Super Bowl Sunday has become a popular reason to have a party. Try **Football Cut-Up Cake** or **Dessert Nachos** at halftime.

Clockwise from top left: Candy Cane Cake (page 16), Chocolate Peppermint Pie (page 16), Merry Berry Dessert (page 17)

Chocolate Peppermint Pie
Photo on page 15

- 1 cup crushed chocolate-covered mint-flavored cookies
- 3 tablespoons hot water
- 1 prepared graham cracker crumb crust (6 ounces)
- 4 ounces PHILADELPHIA BRAND Cream Cheese, softened
- $1/3$ cup sugar
- 2 tablespoons milk
- $1/4$ teaspoon peppermint extract
- 1 tub (8 ounces) COOL WHIP Whipped Topping, thawed
- 6 to 10 drops green food coloring
- Additional thawed COOL WHIP Whipped Topping
- Green gumdrop spearmint leaves (optional)
- Red cinnamon candies (optional)

MIX cookies and hot water in small bowl. Spread evenly in bottom of crust.

BEAT cream cheese in large bowl with electric mixer on medium speed until smooth. Gradually beat in sugar, milk and peppermint extract until well blended. Gently stir in whipped topping. Divide mixture in half; stir food coloring into $1/2$ of the whipped topping mixture until evenly colored. Spoon green and white whipped topping mixtures alternately into crust. Smooth top with spatula.

REFRIGERATE 3 hours or until set. Garnish with additional whipped topping before serving. Decorate with spearmint leaves and cinnamon candies to make holly leaves and berries. Store leftover pie in refrigerator.
Makes 8 servings

Candy Cane Cake
Photo on page 15

- 1 package (9 ounces) chocolate wafer cookies
- 3 tablespoons (about) milk
- 1 tub (8 ounces) COOL WHIP Whipped Topping, thawed
- BAKER'S ANGEL FLAKE Coconut (optional)
- Red and green food colorings (optional)
- Red string licorice (optional)

BRUSH cookies with milk; spread with whipped topping, using about 2 cups. (Refrigerate remaining whipped topping.) Stack cookies in groups of 4 or 5. Place stacks on plastic wrap to form a roll, pressing together lightly. Bend top of roll to form a "cane." Wrap in plastic wrap.

REFRIGERATE at least 6 hours or freeze 4 hours until firm. Just before serving, unwrap and place on serving plate.

FROST with remaining whipped topping. Garnish with coconut tinted with red and green food colorings (see page 9 for directions) and pieces of licorice. To serve, cut cake diagonally into slices. Store leftover cake in refrigerator. *Makes 8 servings*

Merry Berry Desserts
Photo on page 15

1/2 cup sliced strawberries
  and/or banana
1 package (4-serving size)
  JELL-O Brand Strawberry
  Flavor Gelatin
1 cup boiling water
1 cup cold water
1 ripe banana, cut up
1 tub (8 ounces) COOL WHIP
  Whipped Topping,
  thawed

ARRANGE strawberry and/or banana slices in bottoms of 6 muffin cups. Dissolve gelatin completely in boiling water in medium bowl. Stir in cold water. Spoon 3 tablespoons of the gelatin into each muffin cup. Refrigerate until set but not firm.

PLACE remaining gelatin and banana in blender container; cover. Blend on high speed 1 minute. Add 1 1/2 cups of the whipped topping; cover. Blend until well mixed. Spoon over clear gelatin.

REFRIGERATE 4 hours or until firm. To unmold, run small metal spatula around edge of each muffin cup. Dip pan into warm water, just to rim, for about 10 seconds. Place moistened tray on top of pan. Invert; holding pan and tray together, shake slightly to loosen. Gently remove pan. Place desserts on individual serving plates. Garnish with remaining whipped topping.
Makes 6 servings

German Sweet Chocolate Pie

1 package (4 ounces)
  BAKER'S GERMAN'S
  Sweet Chocolate
1/3 cup milk
4 ounces PHILADELPHIA
  BRAND Cream Cheese,
  softened
2 tablespoons sugar
1 tub (8 ounces) COOL WHIP
  Whipped Topping,
  thawed
1 prepared graham cracker
  crumb crust (6 ounces)
  Chocolate Curls (see page 10
  for directions) (optional)

MICROWAVE chocolate and 2 tablespoons of the milk in large microwavable bowl on HIGH 1 1/2 to 2 minutes or until chocolate is almost melted, stirring halfway through heating time. Stir until chocolate is completely melted.

BEAT in cream cheese, sugar and remaining milk until well blended. Refrigerate about 10 minutes to cool. Gently stir in whipped topping until smooth. Spoon into crust.

FREEZE 4 hours or until firm. Garnish with chocolate curls, if desired. Let stand at room temperature 15 minutes or until pie can be cut easily. Store leftover pie in freezer.   *Makes 8 servings*

Christmas Ornament Dessert

The perfect complement to all your holiday parties.

- **7 slices pound cake ($^1/_2$ inch thick)**
- **1 tub (8 ounces) COOL WHIP Whipped Topping, thawed**
- **1 quart strawberry ice cream (4 cups), softened**
- **Multi-colored sprinkles**

LINE 1$^1/_2$-quart bowl with plastic wrap. Place 1 cake slice in bottom and 5 cake slices around side of bowl.

STIR 2$^1/_2$ cups of the whipped topping into ice cream in large bowl. Spoon into cake-lined bowl. Top with remaining cake slice. Cover with plastic wrap.

FREEZE 4 hours or overnight until firm. Invert dessert onto serving plate; remove plastic wrap. Garnish with remaining whipped topping and sprinkles. Let stand at room temperature 15 minutes or until dessert can be cut easily. Store leftover dessert in freezer.

Makes 8 servings

Chocolate Peanut Butter Truffles

- **1 package (8 squares) BAKER'S Semi-Sweet Chocolate**
- **$^1/_2$ cup peanut butter**
- **1 tub (8 ounces) COOL WHIP Whipped Topping, thawed**
- **Powdered sugar, finely chopped nuts, BAKER'S ANGEL FLAKE Coconut, unsweetened cocoa or multi-colored sprinkles**

MICROWAVE chocolate in large microwavable bowl on HIGH 2 minutes or until chocolate is almost melted, stirring halfway through heating time. Stir until chocolate is completely melted.

STIR in peanut butter until smooth. Cool to room temperature. Stir in whipped topping.

REFRIGERATE 1 hour. Shape into 1-inch balls. Roll in powdered sugar, nuts, coconut, cocoa or sprinkles. Store in refrigerator.

Makes about 3 dozen

Cool Christmas Fudge: Prepare as directed above, substituting 4 ounces PHILADELPHIA BRAND Cream Cheese for peanut butter. Stir in $^1/_2$ cup chopped nuts with whipped topping. Spread in foil-lined 8-inch square pan. Refrigerate 4 hours or until firm. Remove from pan. Cut into squares. Store in refrigerator. Makes about 4 dozen.

Top to bottom: Christmas Ornament Dessert, Chocolate Peanut Butter Truffles

Mandarin Mirror

1 package (4-serving size)
   JELL-O Brand Orange
   Flavor Gelatin
1 cup boiling water
1 cup cold water
1/2 cup cold milk
1 package (4-serving size)
   JELL-O French Vanilla or
   Vanilla Flavor Instant
   Pudding and Pie Filling
1 tub (12 ounces)
   COOL WHIP Whipped
   Topping, thawed
14 gingersnap cookies
   Mandarin orange sections
   (optional)

DISSOLVE gelatin completely in boiling water in large bowl. Stir in cold water. Pour 3/4 cup of the gelatin into 9-inch round cake pan which has been sprayed with no stick cooking spray. Refrigerate until set but not firm.

POUR milk into cooled remaining gelatin. Add pudding mix. Beat with wire whisk 1 to 2 minutes. Gently stir in 3 1/2 cups of the whipped topping. Spoon over clear gelatin. Arrange cookies on whipped topping mixture to form "crust." Cover with plastic wrap.

REFRIGERATE 4 hours or until firm. To unmold, run small metal spatula around edge of pan. Dip pan into warm water, just to rim, for about 10 seconds. Place moistened serving plate on top of pan. Invert; holding pan and plate together, shake slightly to loosen. Gently remove pan. Garnish with remaining whipped topping and orange sections.

Makes 8 to 10 servings

Eggnog Trifle

1 1/4 cups cold milk
1 package (4-serving size)
   JELL-O French Vanilla or
   Vanilla Flavor Instant
   Pudding and Pie Filling
4 tablespoons orange juice
1/8 teaspoon ground nutmeg
1 tub (8 ounces) COOL WHIP
   Whipped Topping,
   thawed
1 package (12 ounces)
   ENTENMANN'S All Butter
   Pound Loaf
3 cups halved strawberries
1/4 cup toasted sliced almonds

POUR milk into large bowl. Add pudding mix, 2 tablespoons of the juice and nutmeg. Beat with wire whisk 1 to 2 minutes. Let stand 5 minutes. Gently stir in whipped topping.

SLICE cake horizontally into 4 layers. Sprinkle cake layers evenly with remaining 2 tablespoons juice. Cut into 1-inch cubes.

PLACE 2/3 of the cake cubes in bottom of 2 1/2-quart straight-sided bowl. Spoon 2/3 of the whipped topping mixture over cake cubes. Top with strawberries and toasted almonds (see page 8 for directions), reserving several for garnish, if desired. Layer remaining cake cubes and whipped topping mixture over strawberries. Garnish with reserved strawberries and almonds.

REFRIGERATE at least 1 hour or until ready to serve.

Makes 10 servings

Top to bottom: Eggnog Trifle,
Mandarin Mirror

*Snacks are often a dieter's worst enemy. With the help of **COOL WHIP LITE Whipped Topping**, you'll be ready for your next snack attack.*

Peaches and Cream Dessert

**3 cups frozen sliced
        peaches, thawed
4 tablespoons sugar
1 cup light sour cream
1/4 teaspoon ground
        cinnamon
1 1/2 cups thawed COOL WHIP
        LITE Whipped Topping
1 cup granola cereal
        Cinnamon sticks (optional)**

DICE peaches, reserving several slices for garnish, if desired. Mix peaches and 2 tablespoons of the sugar in large serving bowl.

MIX sour cream, remaining 2 tablespoons sugar and cinnamon in another large bowl. Gently stir in whipped topping. Sprinkle 3/4 cup of the granola over peaches. Top with whipped topping mixture.

REFRIGERATE until ready to serve. Sprinkle with remaining 1/4 cup granola. Garnish with additional whipped topping, reserved peach slices and cinnamon sticks.
                Makes 6 to 8 servings

Note: Recipe can be doubled.

Mini Ladyfinger Napoleons

SPLIT ladyfingers; spread bottom halves with **COOL WHIP LITE Whipped Topping**. Top with sliced strawberries. Cover with top halves of ladyfingers to make "sandwiches."

Chocolate Peanut Butter Desserts

**2 tablespoons skim milk
2 tablespoons peanut butter
1 cup thawed COOL WHIP
        LITE Whipped Topping
2 cups cold skim milk
1 package (4-serving size)
        JELL-O Chocolate Flavor
        Sugar Free Instant
        Pudding and Pie Filling**

MIX 2 tablespoons milk into peanut butter in small bowl. Stir in whipped topping.

POUR 2 cups milk into large bowl. Add pudding mix. Beat with wire whisk 1 to 2 minutes. Spoon pudding and whipped topping mixture alternately into 6 parfait glasses.

REFRIGERATE 1 hour or until ready to serve. Garnish with additional whipped topping.
                Makes 6 servings

Clockwise from top: Peaches and Cream Dessert, Chocolate Peanut Butter Desserts, Chocolate Mousse (page 32), Mini Ladyfinger Napoleons

Dessert Nachos

12 whole graham crackers
1 tub (8 ounces) COOL WHIP
   Whipped Topping,
   thawed
1 cup chopped strawberries
1 cup chopped peeled kiwi
1 cup sliced bananas
   Strawberry dessert
   topping

BREAK graham crackers in half. Score each half diagonally with knife; break apart to form triangles.

ARRANGE ½ of the triangles in single layer on serving plates. Spread evenly with ½ of the whipped topping; top with ½ of the fruit. Drizzle with dessert topping. Repeat layers.

REFRIGERATE until ready to serve.   *Makes 6 servings*

Football Cut-Up Cake

1 package (2-layer size) cake
   mix, any flavor except
   angel food
1 tub (8 ounces) COOL WHIP
   Whipped Topping,
   thawed
5 packages (1.4 ounces each)
   chocolate-covered
   English toffee bars,
   chopped
8 KRAFT Caramels, cut in
   half
   Chocolate bar, broken into
   rectangles

PREPARE and bake cake mix as directed on package for 13×9-inch baking pan. Cool 15 minutes; remove from pan. Cool completely on wire rack.

CUT cake as shown in illustration 1. Using small amount of whipped topping to hold pieces together, arrange cake on serving tray as shown in illustration 2.

FROST cake with remaining whipped topping. Decorate sides with chopped candy bars. Arrange caramel halves to resemble bands and chocolate bar rectangles to resemble laces. Store cake in refrigerator.

Makes 12 to 16 servings

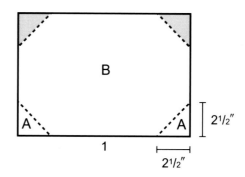

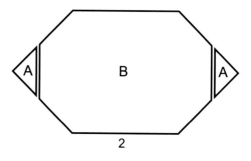

Top to bottom: Football Cut-Up Cake, Dessert Nachos

Cup of Chocolate Dessert

3 1/2 cups small pound cake
   cubes
 1 cup cold milk
 1 cup freshly brewed coffee,
   cooled
 1 package (4-serving size)
   JELL-O Chocolate Flavor
   Instant Pudding and Pie
   Filling
 1 tablespoon sugar
 1 teaspoon ground
   cinnamon
 1 tub (8 ounces) COOL WHIP
   Chocolate Whipped
   Topping, thawed

DIVIDE cake cubes evenly among 6 dessert cups.

PLACE milk, coffee, pudding mix, sugar and cinnamon in blender container; cover. Blend on medium speed 1 to 2 minutes. Pour into dessert cups.

REFRIGERATE until ready to serve. Garnish with whipped topping before serving.
Makes 6 servings

Snowballs

 1 tub (12 ounces)
   COOL WHIP Whipped
   Topping, thawed
24 baked cupcakes, cooled
 8 cups BAKER'S ANGEL
   FLAKE Coconut

SPREAD whipped topping on bottom and sides of cupcakes, holding cupcakes, top side down, in palm of hand. Press coconut into whipped topping. Place cupcakes, top side down, on serving plate.

REFRIGERATE until ready to serve.   *Makes 24*

Tropical Expressions

 1 package (8 ounces)
   PHILADELPHIA BRAND
   Cream Cheese, softened
1/3 cup sugar
 1 package (4-serving size)
   JELL-O French Vanilla or
   Vanilla Flavor Instant
   Pudding and Pie Filling
 1 can (20 ounces) crushed
   pineapple in juice,
   undrained
 1 cup cold milk
 1 tub (8 ounces) COOL WHIP
   Whipped Topping,
   thawed
   BAKER'S ANGEL FLAKE
   Coconut, toasted (see
   page 9 for directions)
   (optional)

BEAT cream cheese in large bowl with electric mixer on medium speed until smooth. Gradually beat in sugar. Add pudding mix, pineapple with juice and milk; beat on low speed until blended.

STIR in 2 cups of the whipped topping. Spoon into 8 dessert glasses.

REFRIGERATE until ready to serve. Garnish with remaining whipped topping and toasted coconut. *Makes 8 servings*

Clockwise from top: Tropical Expressions, Snowballs, Cup of Chocolate Dessert

Chocolate Strawberry Hearts

1 package (15 ounces) ENTENMANN'S Chocolate Pound Cake
2²/₃ cups halved strawberries
1 tub (8 ounces) COOL WHIP Chocolate Whipped Topping, thawed

CUT cake into 16 slices. Place 8 of the slices on individual dessert plates. Cut remaining cake slices with heart-shaped cookie cutter.

SPOON ¹/₃ cup strawberries over each cake slice. Top each with ¹/₃ cup whipped topping.

PLACE heart-shaped cake slice over whipped topping. Garnish with additional strawberries. Serve immediately.   *Makes 8 servings*

Candy Box Heart

1 package (2-layer size) cake mix, any flavor except angel food
1 tub (8 ounces) COOL WHIP Chocolate Whipped Topping, thawed
Chocolate candies

HEAT oven to 325°F.

PREPARE cake mix as directed on package. Divide batter evenly between greased and floured 8-inch round and 8-inch square baking pans. Bake 40 to 45 minutes or until toothpick inserted in centers comes out clean. Cool 10 minutes; remove from pans. Cool completely on wire racks.

LEAVE square cake whole; cut round cake in half as shown in illustration. Using small amount of whipped topping to hold pieces together, arrange cake on serving tray as shown in photograph.

FROST cake with remaining whipped topping. Pipe additional whipped topping around edges of cake (see page 7 for directions), if desired. Decorate with candies. Store cake in refrigerator.
Makes 12 to 16 servings

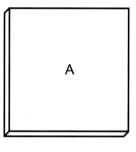

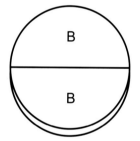

Top to bottom: Candy Box Heart, Chocolate Strawberry Hearts

Black Forest Torte

Even after a long day of shopping, there's still time to make dessert!

2 baked 9-inch round devil's food or chocolate cake layers, cooled
¼ cup almond- or cherry-flavored liqueur or orange juice
1 tub (8 ounces) COOL WHIP Whipped Topping, thawed
1 can (21 ounces) cherry pie filling

SPRINKLE cake layers with liqueur or orange juice.

SPOON or pipe ½ cup whipped topping into 3-inch circle in center of 1 cake layer on serving plate. Spoon or pipe 1 cup of the whipped topping around top edge of cake layer. Spoon ½ of the pie filling between circle and border.

PLACE second cake layer on top. Spoon or pipe remaining whipped topping around top edge of cake layer. Spoon remaining pie filling in center.

REFRIGERATE 1 hour or until ready to serve.

Makes 12 servings

Note: Torte is best made and served the same day. Store leftover torte in refrigerator.

Cherries Jubilee

1¼ cups cold milk
¼ teaspoon almond extract (optional)
1 package (4-serving size) JELL-O Vanilla Flavor Instant Pudding and Pie Filling
1 tub (8 ounces) COOL WHIP Whipped Topping, thawed
¾ cup cherry pie filling

POUR milk and almond extract into large bowl. Add pudding mix. Beat with wire whisk 1 to 2 minutes.

STIR in 2 cups of the whipped topping. Spoon whipped topping mixture and pie filling alternately into 6 parfait glasses.

REFRIGERATE until ready to serve. Garnish with remaining whipped topping.

Makes 6 servings

Top to bottom: Cherries Jubilee,
Black Forest Torte

St. Patrick's Parfaits

They'll all be wearing the green with this fun-to-make, fun-to-eat dessert.

2 cups cold milk
1 package (4-serving size) JELL-O Pistachio Flavor Instant Pudding and Pie Filling
Chocolate sauce
2 cups thawed COOL WHIP Whipped Topping
Chocolate shamrock cutouts (see page 11 for directions) (optional)

POUR milk into large bowl. Add pudding mix. Beat with wire whisk 1 to 2 minutes.

LAYER pudding, chocolate sauce and 1 cup of the whipped topping alternately in 4 parfait glasses. Garnish with remaining whipped topping and chocolate shamrock cutouts.

REFRIGERATE until ready to serve.   *Makes 4 servings*

Chocolate Mousse
Photo on page 22

Chocolate mousse on a diet? You bet, when it's made with this recipe.

1½ cups cold skim milk
1 package (4-serving size) JELL-O Chocolate Sugar Free Instant Pudding and Pie Filling
1½ cups thawed COOL WHIP LITE Whipped Topping
¼ cup fresh raspberries (optional)

POUR milk into large bowl. Add pudding mix. Beat with wire whisk 1 to 2 minutes.

STIR in 1 cup of the whipped topping. Spoon into serving bowl or individual dessert dishes.

REFRIGERATE until ready to serve. Garnish with remaining whipped topping and raspberries.
          Makes 5 servings

Spring Sensations

Fresh air, blossoming flowers and the first warm day signals the arrival of spring and a calendar full of special occasions.

Mark the arrival of spring with friends and an informal Sunday brunch including **Boston Cream Croissants, Dessert Waffles** and **Heavenly Ambrosia in a Cloud.**

Colored eggs and jelly beans mean a visit from the Easter Bunny. Why not make a **Hippity Hop Bunny Cake** to celebrate his arrival?

Surprise your mother with a stunning **Lemon Berry Charlotte** on her Sunday in May.

While the berries of the season are at their luscious peak, you'll want to try several of our easy-to-prepare **Berry Shortcake Shortcuts.**

Clockwise from top left: Heavenly Ambrosia in a Cloud (page 41), Dessert Waffle (page 43), Boston Cream Croissants (page 48)

Come for Brunch

Easter Bonnet Cake

1 package (2-layer size)
    yellow cake mix
1 1/2 cups cold milk
1 package (4-serving size)
    JELL-O Lemon Flavor
    Instant Pudding and Pie
    Filling
1 tub (8 ounces) COOL WHIP
    Whipped Topping,
    thawed
2 2/3 cups (7 ounces) BAKER'S
    ANGEL FLAKE Coconut
    Cloth ribbon (optional)
    Gumdrop Flowers (see
    page 13 for directions)
    (optional)

HEAT oven to 350°F.

PREPARE cake mix as directed on package. Pour 3 1/2 cups of the batter into greased and floured 1 1/2-quart metal or ovenproof glass bowl. Pour remaining batter into greased and floured 12×3/4-inch pizza pan. Bake 15 minutes for the pan and 50 minutes for the bowl or until toothpick inserted in centers comes out clean. Cool 10 minutes; remove from pan and bowl. Cool completely on wire racks. If bottom of bowl-shaped cake is very rounded, thinly slice to make flat. Cut bowl-shaped cake horizontally into 3 layers.

POUR milk into small bowl. Add pudding mix. Beat with wire whisk 1 to 2 minutes.

PLACE 12-inch cake layer on serving tray. Spread with 1 1/2 cups of the whipped topping. Center bottom layer of bowl-shaped cake on frosted layer; spread with 2/3 of the pudding. Add second layer; spread with remaining pudding. Add top layer, forming the crown.

SPREAD remaining whipped topping over the crown. Sprinkle coconut over cake. Tie ribbon around the crown to form hat band. Garnish with Gumdrop Flowers. Store cake in refrigerator.
Makes 16 servings

Cannoli Parfaits

1 cup ricotta cheese
1/3 cup powdered sugar
1 to 2 teaspoons grated
    orange peel
2 tablespoons orange juice
1 1/2 teaspoons vanilla
1 tub (8 ounces) COOL WHIP
    Whipped Topping,
    thawed
1/4 cup chopped dried
    apricots
1/4 cup BAKER'S Semi-Sweet
    Real Chocolate Chips
1/4 cup raisins
10 thin crisp butter cookies,
    coarsely chopped (about
    3/4 cup)

MIX cheese, sugar, orange peel, juice and vanilla in medium bowl. Gently stir in 2 cups of the whipped topping.

STIR in apricots, chips and raisins. Layer cookies and whipped topping mixture alternately in 6 parfait glasses.

REFRIGERATE at least 1 hour or until ready to serve. Garnish with remaining whipped topping.
Makes 6 servings

Top to bottom: Easter Bonnet Cake, Cannoli Parfaits

An Easter Gathering

Hippity Hop Bunny Cake

Surprise the kids after the Easter egg hunt with this cake.

**2 1/4 cups BAKER'S ANGEL
    FLAKE Coconut
    Red food coloring
2 baked 9-inch round cake
    layers, cooled
1 tub (8 ounces) COOL WHIP
    Whipped Topping,
    thawed
    Assorted candies**

TINT 1/4 cup of the coconut pink using red food coloring (see page 9 for directions).

LEAVE 1 cake layer whole; cut remaining cake layer as shown in illustration. Using small amount of whipped topping to hold pieces together, arrange cake on serving tray as shown in photograph.

FROST cake with remaining whipped topping. Sprinkle center of bunny's ears with pink coconut. Sprinkle remaining 2 cups white coconut over bunny's head and outer edges of ears. Decorate with candies. Store cake in refrigerator.
    Makes 12 to 16 servings

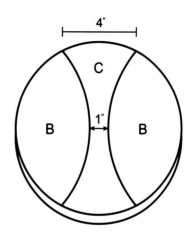

Lemon Berry Charlotte

Any mother would love this stunning dessert.

    1 package (8-serving size) or
       2 packages (4-serving
       size) JELL-O Brand
       Lemon Flavor Gelatin
 1 ½ cups boiling water
    ¾ cup cold water
       Ice cubes
    1 tub (12 ounces)
       COOL WHIP Whipped
       Topping, thawed
    1 cup chopped strawberries
    1 package (3 ounces)
       ladyfingers, split
       Cloth ribbon (optional)
       Strawberry halves
       (optional)
       Fresh mint leaves
       (optional)

DISSOLVE gelatin completely in boiling water in large bowl. Mix cold water and ice to make 1¾ cups. Add to gelatin, stirring until ice is melted. Refrigerate 10 minutes or until slightly thickened, if necessary.

STIR in 3½ cups of the whipped topping and strawberries. Spoon into 2-quart saucepan (about 3½ inches deep) which has been lined with plastic wrap.

REFRIGERATE 4 hours or until firm. Invert saucepan onto serving plate; remove plastic wrap. Spread top and sides of dessert with 1 cup of the whipped topping.

PRESS cut sides of ladyfingers into sides of dessert. Tie ribbon around dessert. Garnish with remaining whipped topping, strawberry halves and mint leaves. Store leftover dessert in refrigerator.   *Makes 12 servings*

Heavenly Ambrosia in a Cloud
Photo on page 35

    1 tub (8 ounces) COOL WHIP
       Whipped Topping,
       thawed
    2 cans (11 ounces each)
       mandarin orange
       sections, drained
    1 can (20 ounces) crushed
       pineapple, drained
    3 cups KRAFT Miniature
       Marshmallows
    2 cups BAKER'S ANGEL
       FLAKE Coconut
       Toasted sliced almonds
       (see page 8 for
       directions) (optional)

SPREAD whipped topping onto bottom and up sides of 2½-quart serving bowl. Refrigerate.

MIX oranges, pineapple, marshmallows and coconut in large bowl. Spoon into whipped topping-lined bowl.

REFRIGERATE at least 1 hour or until ready to serve. Garnish with almonds.   *Makes 16 servings*

Classic Ambrosia: Gently stir whipped topping into fruit mixture. Refrigerate at least 1 hour or until ready to serve. Stir before serving.

Lemon Berry Charlotte

Dessert Waffles

Photo on page 35

- 12 small frozen Belgian waffles
- 1 package (10 ounces) BIRDS EYE Red Raspberries in a Lite Syrup, thawed
- 3 cups assorted fresh fruit
- 1 tub (8 ounces) COOL WHIP Whipped Topping, thawed

HEAT waffles as directed on package.

PLACE raspberries in blender container; cover. Blend until smooth. Strain to remove seeds, if desired.

SERVE waffles with raspberry sauce, fruit and whipped topping.

Makes 12 servings

Baby Booties

- 4 cups BAKER'S ANGEL FLAKE Coconut
- Assorted food colorings
- 24 baked cupcakes, cooled
- 4 cups thawed COOL WHIP Whipped Topping
- Decorating gel
- Miniature star candies

DIVIDE coconut into 4 (1-cup) portions. Tint each cup of coconut a different color using assorted food colorings (see page 9 for directions).

LEAVE 16 cupcakes whole; cut remaining cupcakes as shown in illustration. Using small amount of the whipped topping to hold pieces together, assemble booties on serving tray as shown in photograph.

FROST booties with remaining whipped topping. Press a different color of coconut into whipped topping on each of 4 booties. Pipe decorating gel on the booties to form shoelaces. Decorate with candies. Store cakes in refrigerator.

Makes 16 servings

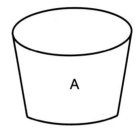

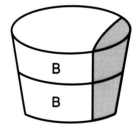

Clockwise from top: Baby Booties, Raspberry Vanilla Pudding Supreme (page 44), Chocolate Truffle Loaf (page 44)

Raspberry Vanilla Pudding Supreme
Photo on page 42

This luscious pudding is perfect for large family parties.

5 1/2 cups cold milk
  4 packages (4-serving size) JELL-O French Vanilla or Vanilla Flavor Instant Pudding and Pie Filling
24 shortbread or vanilla wafer cookies, crumbled (about 1 1/2 cups)
  1 package (10 ounces) BIRDS EYE Raspberries in a Lite Syrup, thawed
1/4 teaspoon red food coloring
  1 tub (8 ounces) COOL WHIP Whipped Topping, thawed
    Fresh raspberries (optional)
    Fresh mint leaves (optional)

POUR 4 cups of the milk into large bowl. Add 2 packages of the pudding mix. Beat with wire whisk 1 to 2 minutes. Spoon into 3-quart serving bowl. Refrigerate 15 minutes. Sprinkle with crumbled cookies.

POUR remaining 1 1/2 cups milk, raspberries in syrup and food coloring into large bowl. Add remaining 2 packages pudding mix. Beat with wire whisk 1 to 2 minutes. Let stand 5 minutes or until slightly thickened. Gently stir in 2 1/2 cups of the whipped topping. Spoon over cookies in bowl.

REFRIGERATE 4 hours or until set. Garnish with remaining whipped topping, fresh raspberries and mint leaves.

Makes 16 servings

Chocolate Truffle Loaf
Photo on page 42

  2 packages (8 squares each) BAKER'S Semi-Sweet Chocolate
1/2 cup (1 stick) margarine or butter
1/4 cup milk
  2 eggs, slightly beaten
  1 teaspoon vanilla
  1 tub (8 ounces) COOL WHIP Whipped Topping, thawed

HEAT 15 squares of the chocolate, margarine and milk in large heavy saucepan on very low heat until chocolate is melted and mixture is smooth, stirring constantly. Stir in eggs with wire whisk; cook 1 minute, stirring constantly. Remove from heat. Stir in vanilla.

REFRIGERATE about 20 minutes or until just cool, stirring occasionally. Gently stir in 2 3/4 cups of the whipped topping. Pour into 8×4-inch loaf pan which has been lined with plastic wrap.

REFRIGERATE 6 hours or overnight or freeze 3 hours until firm. Invert pan onto serving plate; remove plastic wrap. Melt remaining 1 square chocolate; drizzle over dessert (see page 11 for directions). Garnish with remaining whipped topping. Store leftover dessert in refrigerator.

Makes 16 servings

Creamy Lemon Bars

1 1/2 cups graham cracker
    crumbs
  1/2 cup sugar
  1/3 cup margarine or butter,
    melted
  1 package (8 ounces)
    PHILADELPHIA BRAND
    Cream Cheese, softened
  2 tablespoons milk
  1 tub (8 ounces) COOL WHIP
    Whipped Topping,
    thawed
3 1/2 cups cold milk
  2 packages (4-serving size)
    JELL-O Lemon Flavor
    Instant Pudding and Pie
    Filling

MIX graham cracker crumbs,
1/4 cup of the sugar and margarine
in 13×9-inch pan. Press firmly
into bottom of pan. Refrigerate
15 minutes.

BEAT cream cheese, remaining 1/4
cup sugar and 2 tablespoons milk
until smooth. Gently stir in 1/2 of
the whipped topping. Spread over
crust.

POUR 3 1/2 cups cold milk into
large bowl. Add pudding mixes.
Beat with wire whisk 1 to
2 minutes. Pour over cream cheese
layer.

REFRIGERATE 4 hours or
overnight. Spread remaining
whipped topping over pudding
just before serving.
Makes 15 servings

Berries Delight: Prepare as
directed above, using French
vanilla or vanilla flavor pudding
mix. Arrange 2 pints strawberries,
halved, over cream cheese mixture
before topping with pudding.

Strawberry Cool 'n Easy Pie

  1 package (4-serving size)
    JELL-O Brand Strawberry
    Flavor Gelatin
  2/3 cup boiling water
  1/2 cup cold water
    Ice cubes
  1 tub (8 ounces) COOL WHIP
    Whipped Topping,
    thawed
  1 cup chopped strawberries
  1 prepared graham cracker
    crumb crust (6 ounces)

DISSOLVE gelatin completely in
boiling water in large bowl. Mix
cold water and ice to make
1 1/4 cups. Add to gelatin, stirring
until slightly thickened. Remove
any remaining ice.

STIR in whipped topping with
wire whisk until smooth. Mix in
strawberries. Refrigerate 20 to
30 minutes or until mixture is
very thick and will mound. Spoon
into crust.

REFRIGERATE 4 hours or until
firm. Garnish with additional
whipped topping and strawberries.
Store leftover pie in refrigerator.
Makes 8 servings

Lemon Chiffon Pie: Prepare as
directed above, using lemon flavor
gelatin. Add 2 teaspoons grated
lemon peel and 2 tablespoons
lemon juice to dissolved gelatin
with cold water and ice. Garnish
with additional whipped topping
and grated lemon peel or Citrus
Twists (see page 12 for directions).

Strawberry Angel Torte

The strawberry fans give a clue to the fresh berries hidden inside.

- 1 package (14.5 ounces) angel food cake mix
- 1 pint fresh strawberries, crushed
- 1 tablespoon milk
- 1 tub (12 ounces) COOL WHIP Whipped Topping, thawed
- Strawberry Fans (see page 12 for directions) (optional)
- Fresh mint leaves (optional)

PREPARE and bake cake mix as directed on package for 10×4-inch tube pan. Cool and remove from pan as directed. Cut cake horizontally into 3 layers.

STIR strawberries and milk into 1½ cups of the whipped topping in large bowl. Place 1 cake layer on serving plate. Spread with ½ of the strawberry mixture. Repeat layers, ending with top of cake. Frost top and sides of cake with remaining whipped topping.

REFRIGERATE at least 1 hour or until ready to serve. Garnish top and sides of cake with Strawberry Fans and mint leaves. Serve cake with sweetened sliced strawberries, if desired.   *Makes 12 servings*

Berry Shortcake Shortcuts

Celebrate with fruit at the peak of their season using these easy serving suggestions.

Raspberry Shortcake: Top 1 slice pound cake with 1 scoop raspberry sherbet or sorbet. Garnish with dollop of **COOL WHIP Whipped Topping** and fresh raspberries.

Shortcake Dessert: Fill center of 1 sponge cake dessert shell with dollop of **COOL WHIP Whipped Topping**. Garnish with strawberry slices.

"Shortcake" in a Cloud: Spoon ⅓ cup **COOL WHIP Whipped Topping** onto serving plate. Using back of spoon, spread whipped topping to form a depression in center. Refrigerate until ready to serve. Fill with mixture of blueberries, raspberries and strawberries.

Traditional Shortcake: Split and fill 1 biscuit with sweetened berries and **COOL WHIP Whipped Topping**. Garnish with dollop of whipped topping and additional berries.

Clockwise from top right:
Strawberry Angel Torte,
"Shortcake" in a Cloud, Raspberry
Shortcake, Shortcake Dessert

Strawberry Dip

1 tub (8 ounces) COOL WHIP
   LITE Whipped Topping,
   thawed
1 container (8 ounces)
   strawberry flavored
   lowfat yogurt
$1/2$ cup crushed strawberries
1 tablespoon grated orange
   peel
   Assorted fresh fruit, such
   as strawberries, grapes,
   kiwi, sliced oranges or
   pineapple

MIX whipped topping, yogurt,
strawberries and orange peel until
well blended. Spoon into serving
bowl. Refrigerate until ready to
serve.

SERVE as a dip with fresh fruit.
Makes about 5 cups

Boston Cream Croissants
Photo on page 35

$1 1/4$ cups cold milk
1 package (4-serving size)
   JELL-O French Vanilla or
   Vanilla Flavor Instant
   Pudding and Pie Filling
1 cup thawed COOL WHIP
   Whipped Topping
12 miniature croissants
1 square BAKER'S
   Unsweetened Chocolate
1 tablespoon margarine or
   butter
$3/4$ cup powdered sugar
2 tablespoons water

POUR milk into large bowl. Add
pudding mix. Beat with wire
whisk 1 to 2 minutes. Gently stir
in whipped topping.

SPLIT croissants horizontally; fill
with whipped topping mixture.
Refrigerate.

MELT chocolate and margarine in
small heavy saucepan on very low
heat, stirring constantly. Remove
from heat. Stir in sugar and water
until smooth. Drizzle over tops of
croissants.

REFRIGERATE until ready to
serve.   *Makes 12 servings*

Caramel Apple Salad

3 Granny Smith or other
   green apples, diced
3 red apples, diced
6 packages (2.07 ounces
   each) chocolate-covered
   caramel peanut nougat
   bars, chopped
1 tub (8 ounces) COOL WHIP
   Whipped Topping,
   thawed
   Apple slices (optional)

MIX apples and chopped candy
bars until well blended. Gently stir
in whipped topping.

REFRIGERATE 1 hour or until
ready to serve. Garnish with apple
slices.   *Makes 20 servings*

Note: Salad is best made and
served the same day.

*Top to bottom: Caramel Apple
Salad, Strawberry Dip*

Summertime Celebrations

Most of us wish summer celebrations would last all year. Memorial Day signals the unofficial beginning of summer and the first picnic of the season. You'll want to make **Watermelon Slices,** a real crowd-pleaser.

There's nothing more patriotic than the **Stars and Stripes Dessert** for a glorious Fourth of July barbecue or other event celebrating the red, white and blue holiday.

Simply elegant desserts like **Romanoff Tarts** and **Lemon Berry Terrine** are perfect standouts for a garden wedding reception.

An annual event of grand proportions, such as a family reunion, calls for a dessert of grand proportions! **Chocolate Banana Berry Trifle** or **Creamy Orange Cake** will feed a large crowd after a day full of activities.

Watermelon Slices (page 53)

Stars and Stripes Dessert

2 pints strawberries
1 package (12 ounces)
    ENTENMANN'S All Butter
    Pound Loaf, cut into
    8 slices
1⅓ cups blueberries
1 tub (8 ounces) COOL WHIP
    Whipped Topping,
    thawed

SLICE 1 cup of the strawberries; set aside. Halve remaining strawberries; set aside.

LINE bottom of 12×8-inch baking dish with cake slices. Top with 1 cup sliced strawberries, 1 cup of the blueberries and whipped topping.

PLACE strawberry halves and remaining ⅓ cup blueberries on whipped topping to create a flag design.

REFRIGERATE until ready to serve.   *Makes 15 servings*

Watermelon Slices
Photo on page 51

Slices of ice cold "watermelon" are a refreshing summer treat.

1 tub (8 ounces) COOL WHIP
    Whipped Topping,
    thawed
3 to 4 drops green food
    coloring
1 pint raspberry or
    strawberry sherbet or
    sorbet (2 cups), softened
1 square BAKER'S
    Semi-Sweet Chocolate,
    chopped

LINE 1½-quart bowl with plastic wrap. Mix ½ of the whipped topping with food coloring in another large bowl until well blended. Spread on bottom and up sides of prepared bowl. Freeze 30 minutes or until firm.

SPREAD remaining whipped topping over green layer. Freeze 1 hour or until firm.

MIX sherbet and chopped chocolate in medium bowl. Spoon into center of whipped topping.

FREEZE at least 4 hours or overnight until firm. Invert bowl onto serving plate; remove plastic wrap. Let stand at room temperature 5 minutes or until dessert can be cut easily. Cut into slices. Serve immediately. Store leftover dessert in freezer.
                 Makes 10 to 12 servings

Stars and Stripes Dessert

Star Spangled Snack

1 package (4-serving size)
   JELL-O Brand Berry Blue
   Flavor Gelatin
1 package (4-serving size)
   JELL-O Brand Gelatin,
   any red flavor
2 cups boiling water
1 cup cold water
1 tub (8 ounces) COOL WHIP
   Whipped Topping,
   thawed

DISSOLVE each package of
gelatin completely in 1 cup boiling
water in separate bowls. Stir
1/2 cup cold water into each bowl
of gelatin. Pour each mixture into
separate 8-inch square pans.
Refrigerate at least 3 hours or until
firm. Cut gelatin in each pan into
1/2-inch cubes.

SPOON blue cubes evenly into
8 dessert dishes. Cover with
whipped topping. Top with red
cubes. Garnish with remaining
whipped topping.

REFRIGERATE until ready to
serve.   *Makes 8 servings*

4th of July Dessert

1 package (8-serving size) or
   2 packages (4-serving
   size) JELL-O Brand
   Gelatin, any red flavor
2 cups boiling water
2 cups cold water
1 tub (8 ounces) COOL WHIP
   Whipped Topping,
   thawed
1 cup sliced strawberries
1/4 cup blueberries

DISSOLVE gelatin completely in
boiling water in large bowl. Stir in
cold water. Pour into 2-quart
serving bowl. Refrigerate at least
3 hours or until firm.

SPREAD whipped topping over
gelatin. Decorate with strawberries
to create a star design. Sprinkle
with blueberries.

REFRIGERATE until ready to
serve.   *Makes 8 servings*

Firecrackers

5 cups BAKER'S ANGEL
   FLAKE Coconut
   Blue food coloring
24 baked cupcakes, cooled
1 tub (12 ounces)
   COOL WHIP Whipped
   Topping, thawed
   Red decorating gel
   Red string licorice

TINT coconut using blue food
coloring (see page 9).

TRIM any "lips" off top edges of
cupcakes. Using small amount of
whipped topping, attach bottoms
of 2 cupcakes together. Repeat
with remaining cupcakes. Stand
attached cupcakes on 1 end on
serving plate or tray.

FROST with remaining whipped
topping. Press coconut onto sides.

DRAW a star on top of each
firecracker with decorating gel.
Insert pieces of licorice for fuses.
Store cakes in refrigerator.
                        Makes 12

*Clockwise from top: 4th of July
Dessert, Firecrackers, Star
Spangled Snack*

Father's Day Cheesecake Pie

Dad will welcome a slice of this delicious cheesecake after a day of fishing or golf.

1 package (8 ounces) PHILADELPHIA BRAND Cream Cheese, softened
¹/₃ cup sugar
1 teaspoon vanilla
1 tub (8 ounces) COOL WHIP Whipped Topping, thawed
1 prepared graham cracker crumb crust (6 ounces)
   Additional thawed COOL WHIP Whipped Topping (about ¹/₂ cup)
   KRAFT Miniature Marshmallows
   Strawberry dessert topping or jam

BEAT cream cheese, sugar and vanilla with wire whisk in large bowl until smooth. Gently stir in whipped topping. Spoon into crust.

REFRIGERATE at least 4 hours or until set.

DECORATE top of pie with additional whipped topping and marshmallows to resemble a tie. Fill in tie and outline edge of pie with dessert topping. Store leftover pie in refrigerator.

Makes 8 servings

Dessert Grillers

4 cups assorted fruit, such as strawberries, sliced kiwi, oranges or pineapple
12 thin wooden skewers
¹/₂ cup (1 stick) margarine or butter
1 package (12 ounces) ENTENMANN'S All Butter Pound Loaf, cut into 12 slices
2 tablespoons sugar
1 teaspoon ground cinnamon
1 tub (8 ounces) COOL WHIP Whipped Topping, thawed

ARRANGE fruit on skewers; set aside. Heat grill or broiler.

SPREAD margarine evenly on cake slices. Mix sugar and cinnamon in small bowl; sprinkle over cake slices.

PLACE cake slices on grill over hot coals or on rack of broiler pan. Grill or broil on both sides until lightly toasted. Cool. Serve with whipped topping and fruit kabobs. *Makes 12 servings*

Top to bottom: Father's Day Cheesecake Pie, Dessert Grillers, Pistachio Pineapple Delight (page 67)

Lemon Berry Terrine

An easy but elegant dessert for a gala affair.

  1 package (12 ounces)
      ENTENMANN'S All Butter
      Pound Loaf
  1 package (8 ounces)
      PHILADELPHIA BRAND
      Cream Cheese, softened
1 1/2 cups cold milk
  1 package (4-serving size)
      JELL-O Lemon Flavor
      Instant Pudding and Pie
      Filling
  1 teaspoon grated lemon
      peel
  1 tub (8 ounces) COOL WHIP
      Whipped Topping,
      thawed
  1 pint strawberries, hulled

LINE bottom and sides of
8×4-inch loaf pan with wax paper.

CUT rounded top off cake; reserve
for another use. Trim edges of
cake. Cut cake horizontally into
5 slices. Line bottom and long
sides of pan with 3 cake slices.
Cut another cake slice in half;
place on short sides of pan.

BEAT cream cheese and 1/2 cup
of the milk in large bowl with
electric mixer on low speed until
smooth. Add remaining milk,
pudding mix and lemon peel; beat
1 to 2 minutes. Gently stir in
1 cup of the whipped topping.

SPOON 1/2 of the filling into
cake-lined pan. Arrange 1/2 of the
strawberries, stem-side up, in
filling, pressing down slightly. Top
with remaining filling. Place
remaining cake slice on top of
filling.

REFRIGERATE 3 hours or until
firm. Invert pan onto serving
plate; remove wax paper. Garnish
with remaining whipped topping
and strawberries. Store leftover
dessert in refrigerator.

Makes 16 servings

Romanoff Tarts

  1 cup cold milk
  2 tablespoons orange-
      flavored liqueur or
      orange juice
  1 package (4-serving size)
      JELL-O French Vanilla or
      Vanilla Flavor Instant
      Pudding and Pie Filling
  1 cup thawed COOL WHIP
      Whipped Topping
  1 cup chopped strawberries
  6 prepared graham cracker
      tart shells
      Assorted fruit (optional)

POUR milk and liqueur into large
bowl. Add pudding mix. Beat with
wire whisk 1 to 2 minutes.

STIR in whipped topping and
strawberries. Spoon into tart
shells.

REFRIGERATE 1 hour or until
ready to serve. Garnish with
additional whipped topping and
fruit.   *Makes 6 servings*

*Clockwise from top: Romanoff
Tarts, Lemon Berry Terrine,
Strawberry Heart Pillows
(page 66)*

Dessert Pizza

This pizza is lots of fun. Try your favorite combination of fruit and dessert toppings.

  1 package (20 ounces)
      refrigerated chocolate
      chip cookie dough
  2 cups thawed COOL WHIP
      Whipped Topping
  2 cups assorted fruit, such
      as blueberries, halved
      green grapes and sliced
      strawberries
      Strawberry dessert
      topping

HEAT oven to 350°F.

LINE 12-inch pizza pan with foil; grease foil. Press dough into prepared pan. Bake 20 minutes or until golden brown. Cool in pan on wire rack. Remove foil. Place cookie crust on serving plate.

SPREAD whipped topping on cookie crust. Garnish with fruit. Drizzle with dessert topping. Serve immediately or refrigerate until ready to serve.

Makes 12 servings

Strawberry Banana Split Pie

  1 banana, sliced
  1 prepared chocolate flavor
      crumb crust (6 ounces)
  3/4 cup cold milk or
      half-and-half
  3/4 cup pureed strawberries
      Red food coloring
  1 package (4-serving size)
      JELL-O Vanilla Flavor
      Instant Pudding and Pie
      Filling
  1 tub (8 ounces) COOL WHIP
      Whipped Topping,
      thawed
      Sliced bananas and
      strawberries
      Chocolate dessert topping
      Additional thawed
      COOL WHIP Whipped
      Topping
  1 maraschino cherry

ARRANGE banana slices in bottom of crust.

POUR milk, strawberry puree and food coloring into large bowl. Add pudding mix. Beat with wire whisk 1 to 2 minutes. Let stand 5 minutes. Gently stir in whipped topping. Spoon into crust.

FREEZE 6 hours or overnight until firm. Let stand at room temperature 15 minutes or until pie can be cut easily.

GARNISH with sliced bananas and strawberries. Drizzle with dessert topping. Top with dollop of additional whipped topping and cherry. Store leftover pie in freezer. *Makes 8 servings*

Clockwise from top left: Chocolate Caramel Parfaits (page 66), Dessert Pizza, Strawberry Banana Split Pie

Creamy Orange Cake

1 can (6 ounces) frozen orange juice concentrate, thawed
1 package (2-layer size) yellow cake mix
1 package (3 ounces) PHILADELPHIA BRAND Cream Cheese, softened
¼ cup sugar
1 tub (12 ounces) COOL WHIP Whipped Topping, thawed
  Mandarin orange sections (optional)
  Fresh mint leaves (optional)

POUR concentrate into 2-cup measuring cup, reserving 2 tablespoons for cake filling. Add enough water to remaining concentrate to make the amount of liquid needed for cake mix. Prepare cake mix as directed on package, using measured liquid. Pour into 2 greased and floured 9-inch round cake pans. Bake and cool as directed on package.

BEAT cream cheese and sugar in large bowl with electric mixer on low speed until smooth. Beat in reserved concentrate. Gently stir in ½ cup of the whipped topping.

PLACE 1 cake layer on serving plate. Spread with cream cheese mixture. Top with second cake layer. Frost cake with remaining whipped topping. Pipe additional whipped topping around bottom of cake (see page 7 for directions), if desired. Garnish with orange sections and mint leaves. Store cake in refrigerator.

Makes 12 to 16 servings

Lemon Cheese Squares

15 whole graham crackers, broken in half
2 packages (8 ounces each) PHILADELPHIA BRAND Cream Cheese, softened
3 cups cold milk
2 packages (6-serving size) JELL-O Lemon Flavor Instant Pudding and Pie Filling
1 tub (8 ounces) COOL WHIP Whipped Topping, thawed
1 can (21 ounces) blueberry pie filling or Citrus Twists (see page 12)

ARRANGE ½ of the crackers in bottom of 13×9-inch pan, cutting crackers to fit, if necessary.

BEAT cream cheese in large bowl with electric mixer on low speed until smooth. Gradually beat in 1 cup of the milk. Add remaining milk and pudding mixes. Beat 1 to 2 minutes. Gently stir in 2 cups of the whipped topping.

SPREAD ½ of the pudding mixture over crackers. Add second layer of crackers; top with remaining pudding mixture and whipped topping.

FREEZE 2 hours or until firm. Let stand at room temperature 15 minutes or until squares can be cut easily. Garnish with pie filling. Store leftover dessert in freezer.

Makes 18 servings

Clockwise from top: Chocolate Banana Berry Trifle (page 66), Creamy Orange Cake, Lemon Cheese Squares

Lemonade Stand Pie

1 can (6 ounces) frozen
    lemonade or pink
    lemonade concentrate,
    partially thawed
1 pint vanilla ice cream
    (2 cups), softened
1 tub (8 ounces) COOL WHIP
    Whipped Topping,
    thawed
1 prepared graham cracker
    crumb crust (6 ounces)
    Citrus Twists (see page 12
    for directions) (optional)
    Fresh mint leaves
    (optional)

BEAT concentrate in large bowl with electric mixer on low speed about 30 seconds. Gradually spoon in ice cream; beat until well blended. Gently stir in whipped topping until smooth. Freeze until mixture will mound, if necessary. Spoon into crust.

FREEZE 4 hours or overnight until firm. Let stand at room temperature 15 minutes or until pie can be cut easily.

GARNISH with Citrus Twists and mint leaves. Store leftover pie in freezer. *Makes 8 servings*

Summer Lime Pie

1 package (4-serving size)
    JELL-O Brand Lime
    Flavor Gelatin
$2/3$ cup boiling water
$1/2$ teaspoon grated lime peel
3 tablespoons lime juice
$1/2$ cup cold water
    Ice cubes
1 tub (8 ounces) COOL WHIP
    Whipped Topping,
    thawed
1 prepared graham cracker
    crumb crust (6 ounces)
    Lime slices, cut into
    quarters (optional)

DISSOLVE gelatin completely in boiling water in large bowl. Stir in lime peel and juice. Mix cold water and ice to make $1\,1/4$ cups. Add to gelatin, stirring until ice is melted.

STIR in whipped topping with wire whisk until smooth. Refrigerate 10 to 15 minutes or until mixture is very thick and will mound. Spoon into crust.

REFRIGERATE 2 hours or until firm. Garnish with additional whipped topping and lime slices. Store leftover pie in refrigerator.
Makes 8 servings

Clockwise from top: Lemonade Stand Pie, Frozen Strawberry-Yogurt Pie (page 67), Summer Lime Pie

Chocolate Banana Berry Trifle
Photo on page 63

>   1 package (20 to 23 ounces) brownie mix
>   2 cups sliced strawberries
>   2 bananas, sliced
>   4 packages (1.4 ounces each) chocolate-covered English toffee bars, chopped
>   2 tubs (8 ounces) COOL WHIP Chocolate Whipped Topping, thawed

PREPARE and bake brownie mix as directed on package. Cool completely in pan on wire rack. Cut into ½-inch squares.

LAYER ½ of the brownies, strawberries, bananas, chopped candy bars and whipped topping in 4-quart serving bowl. Repeat layers.

REFRIGERATE at least 1 hour or until ready to serve. Garnish with additional chopped candy bars, if desired. *Makes 16 servings*

Strawberry Heart Pillows
Photo on page 59

>   1 frozen ready-to-bake puff pastry sheet
>   1 cup strawberry jam or preserves
>   1 tub (8 ounces) COOL WHIP Whipped Topping, thawed
>   Sliced strawberries

THAW pastry as directed on package. Heat oven to 350°F. Unfold pastry. Using 2-inch heart-shaped cookie cutter, cut into 16 hearts. Or, using sharp knife, cut into 30 (1½-inch) squares. Place on ungreased cookie sheets.

BAKE 20 minutes or until golden. Remove from cookie sheets. Cool completely on wire racks. Split each pastry horizontally in half.

SPREAD 1 teaspoon jam on bottom half of each heart. Top with dollop of whipped topping. Cover with top half of heart. Garnish with whipped topping and strawberries.

REFRIGERATE until ready to serve.
Makes 16 hearts or 30 squares

Chocolate Caramel Parfaits
Photo on page 60

>   28 chocolate sandwich cookies, crushed (2 cups)
>   1 tub (8 ounces) COOL WHIP Chocolate Whipped Topping, thawed
>   1 cup caramel sauce or dessert topping
>   ½ cup hot fudge dessert topping
>   1 cup chopped pecans

LAYER crushed cookies, 2½ cups of the whipped topping, dessert toppings and pecans in 4 (8-ounce) dessert glasses.

REFRIGERATE at least 1 hour or until ready to serve. Garnish with remaining whipped topping.
Makes 4 servings

Pistachio Pineapple Delight
Photo on page 56

    1 package (4-serving size)
        JELL-O Pistachio Flavor
        Instant Pudding and Pie
        Filling
    1 can (20 ounces) crushed
        pineapple in syrup
    1 cup KRAFT Miniature
        Marshmallows
    1/2 cup chopped nuts
    1 3/4 cups thawed COOL WHIP
        Whipped Topping
        Sliced strawberries
        (optional)

STIR pudding mix, pineapple, marshmallows and nuts in large bowl until well blended. Gently stir in whipped topping.

REFRIGERATE 1 hour or until ready to serve. Garnish with additional whipped topping and sliced strawberries.
Makes 8 servings

Frozen Strawberry-Yogurt Pie
Photo on page 64

    2 containers (8 ounces each)
        vanilla or strawberry
        flavored yogurt
    1 tub (8 ounces) COOL WHIP
        Whipped Topping,
        thawed
    2 cups sweetened chopped
        strawberries
    1 prepared graham cracker
        crumb crust (6 ounces)

STIR yogurt gently into whipped topping until well blended. Stir in strawberries. Spoon into crust.

FREEZE 4 hours or overnight until firm. Let stand in refrigerator 15 minutes or until pie can be cut easily.

GARNISH with additional whipped topping and whole strawberries. Store leftover pie in freezer.   *Makes 8 servings*

Cookies and Cream Pie

    1 1/2 cups cold milk or
        half-and-half
    1 package (4-serving size)
        JELL-O Vanilla Flavor
        Instant Pudding and Pie
        Filling
    1 tub (8 ounces) COOL WHIP
        Whipped Topping,
        thawed
    1 cup chopped chocolate
        sandwich cookies
    1 prepared chocolate flavor
        crumb crust (6 ounces)

POUR milk into large bowl. Add pudding mix. Beat with wire whisk 1 to 2 minutes. Let stand 5 minutes. Gently stir in whipped topping and chopped cookies. Spoon into crust.

FREEZE 6 hours or overnight until firm. Let stand at room temperature 15 minutes or until pie can be cut easily.

GARNISH with additional chocolate sandwich cookies, if desired. Store leftover pie in freezer.   *Makes 8 servings*

Autumn Delights

The cool, crisp air and wonderful, warm colors of autumn are so inviting you'll look for any reason to plan an event to bring family and friends together.

When the kids go back to school, surprise them with a variety of after school treats such as **Monkey Bars, Peanut Pockets** or **Ice Cream Cone Cakes.** And, you'll want to make sure that **Boo the Ghost** makes a special appearance for Halloween.

Try one of our chocolate recipes for your next fall get-together. **Chocolate Cookie Parfaits, Candy Bar Pie** or **Chocolate Tornado** is sure to please the most discriminating chocolate lover.

When it's time for America's oldest celebration, **Double Layer Pumpkin Pie** or **Cranberry Raspberry Mousse** makes a grand finale to your traditional Thanksgiving menu.

Top to bottom: Caramel Apple Squares (page 80), Apple Crunch (page 80)

Peanut Pockets

9 graham cracker squares
6 squares BAKER'S
   Semi-Sweet Chocolate
1/4 cup milk
1 cup creamy peanut butter
2 tablespoons margarine or
   butter
1 tub (8 ounces) COOL WHIP
   Whipped Topping,
   thawed
1/3 cup peanuts

ARRANGE crackers in bottom of foil-lined 8-inch square pan, cutting crackers to fit, if necessary.

MICROWAVE chocolate and milk in medium microwavable bowl on HIGH 1 to 2 minutes or until chocolate is almost melted, stirring halfway through heating time. Stir until chocolate is completely melted. Reserve 2 tablespoons for garnish; set aside. Spread remaining chocolate mixture evenly over crackers. Freeze 10 minutes or until firm.

MICROWAVE peanut butter and margarine in large microwavable bowl on HIGH 30 seconds or until margarine is melted. Stir until well blended. Gently stir in whipped topping. Spread evenly over chocolate layer. With back of spoon, make indentations in whipped topping mixture at 1-inch intervals. Place 1 peanut in each "pocket." Drizzle with reserved chocolate mixture. (Reheat chocolate until melted, if necessary.)

REFRIGERATE 4 hours or overnight until firm. Cut into small squares. Store in refrigerator.
Makes 36

Monkey Bars

28 chocolate sandwich
   cookies, finely chopped
   (2 cups)
1/4 cup (1/2 stick) margarine or
   butter
1 package (8 ounces)
   PHILADELPHIA BRAND
   Cream Cheese, softened
1/4 cup sugar
1 tablespoon milk
1 tub (8 ounces) COOL WHIP
   Chocolate Whipped
   Topping, thawed
1 large banana, chopped
   Banana slices (optional)

MICROWAVE 1 1/2 cups of the chopped cookies and margarine in medium microwavable bowl on HIGH 1 minute or until margarine is melted. Stir until well mixed. Press firmly into bottom of foil-lined 8-inch square pan.

BEAT cream cheese, sugar and milk in large bowl until smooth. Gently stir in 2 cups of the whipped topping and chopped banana. Spread over crust. Sprinkle with remaining 1/2 cup chopped cookies. Spread with remaining whipped topping.

REFRIGERATE 4 hours or overnight until firm. Cut into squares. Garnish with banana slices. Store in refrigerator.
Makes 12

Clockwise from top: Ice Cream Cone Cakes (page 72), Rainbow Sandwiches (page 75), Peanut Pockets, Monkey Bars

Boo the Ghost

1 baked 13×9-inch cake,
   cooled
1 tub (8 ounces) COOL WHIP
   Whipped Topping,
   thawed
2 chocolate wafer cookies
2 green candy wafers
   Candy corn
1 black jelly bean
   Black or red string licorice

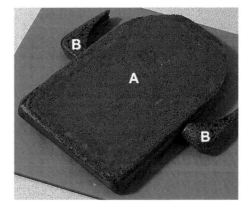

CUT cake as shown in illustration. Using small amount of whipped topping to hold pieces together, arrange cake on serving tray as shown in photograph.

FROST cake with remaining whipped topping. Decorate with cookies and candy wafers for eyes and candy corn for mouth. Make a spider using the jelly bean for its body and pieces of licorice for its legs. Store cake in refrigerator.

Makes 12 to 16 servings

Ice Cream Cone Cakes
Photo on page 70

1 package (2-layer size)
   chocolate or yellow cake
   mix
24 flat-bottom ice cream
   cones
1 tub (8 ounces) COOL WHIP
   Chocolate Whipped
   Topping, thawed
   Multi-colored or chocolate
   sprinkles

HEAT oven to 350°F.

PREPARE cake mix as directed on package. Spoon 2 heaping tablespoons batter into each cone. Place on cookie sheets. Bake 25 minutes or until toothpick inserted in centers comes out clean. Cool on wire rack.

SPOON or pipe whipped topping onto cones to resemble ice cream. Garnish with sprinkles. Refrigerate until ready to serve.   *Makes 24*

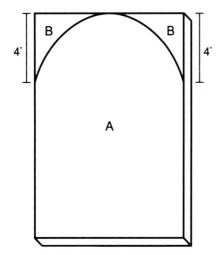

Top to bottom: Crazy Colored
Halloween Desserts (page 75),
Boo the Ghost

Chocolate Cookie Parfaits

14 chocolate sandwich
    cookies, crushed (1 cup)
1 tub (8 ounces) COOL WHIP
    Chocolate Whipped
    Topping, thawed

LAYER crushed cookies alternately with whipped topping in 4 (6-ounce) dessert glasses, ending with whipped topping.

REFRIGERATE at least 1 hour or until ready to serve. Garnish with additional whipped topping and cookies.   *Makes 4 servings*

Mint Chocolate Cookie Parfaits: Mix 4 chopped chocolate-covered mint patties with crushed cookies before layering with whipped topping.

Crazy Colored Halloween Desserts
Photo on page 73

1 package (8 ounces)
    PHILADELPHIA BRAND
    Cream Cheese, softened
4 scoops KOOL-AID
    Sugar-Sweetened Soft
    Drink Mix, any green or
    orange flavor
1/2 cup milk
1 tub (8 ounces) COOL WHIP
    Whipped Topping,
    thawed
12 sponge cake dessert shells
    Assorted candies and
    cookies

BEAT cream cheese and soft drink mix in large bowl until well blended. Gradually beat in milk until smooth. Gently stir in whipped topping.

SPOON about 1/3 cup whipped topping mixture into each dessert shell. Decorate with candies and cookies to resemble pumpkins, spiders and witches. Refrigerate until ready to serve.
          Makes 12 servings

Rainbow Sandwiches
Photo on page 70

1 package (4-serving size)
    JELL-O Brand Gelatin,
    any flavor
1 cup boiling water
3/4 cup cold water
1 package (12 ounces)
    ENTENMANN'S All Butter
    Pound Loaf, cut into
    1/4-inch slices
    Thawed COOL WHIP
    Whipped Topping

DISSOLVE gelatin completely in boiling water in small bowl. Stir in cold water. Pour into 9-inch square pan. Refrigerate at least 3 hours or until firm. Cut gelatin and cake slices into circles, squares and/or rectangles.

SPREAD whipped topping on cake slices. Place gelatin shapes on 1/2 of the cake slices. Top with remaining cake slices, whipped topping side down.

REFRIGERATE until ready to serve.   *Makes 8 to 12 servings*

Chocolate Cookie Parfait

S'More Squares

1 cup graham cracker
   crumbs
3 tablespoons margarine or
   butter, melted
2 squares BAKER'S
   Semi-Sweet Chocolate
1/4 cup milk
2 cups KRAFT Miniature
   Marshmallows
1 tub (8 ounces) COOL WHIP
   Chocolate Whipped
   Topping, thawed
2/3 cup BAKER'S Semi-Sweet
   Real Chocolate Chips

MIX crumbs and margarine in
small bowl. Press into bottom of
foil-lined 8-inch square pan.

MICROWAVE chocolate squares
and milk in large microwavable
bowl on HIGH 1 to 1 1/2 minutes or
until chocolate is almost melted,
stirring halfway through heating
time. Stir until chocolate is
completely melted.

STIR in marshmallows until
slightly melted. Refrigerate
15 minutes or until cool, stirring
occasionally. Gently stir in
2 1/2 cups of the whipped topping
and 1/3 cup of the chips. Spread
over crust.

SPREAD remaining whipped
topping over top. Sprinkle with
remaining 1/3 cup chips. Garnish
with additional graham cracker
crumbs and marshmallows.

FREEZE 4 hours or overnight
until firm. Cut into squares. Store
in freezer.   *Makes 16*

Chocolate Tornado

*This is an updated version of the
all-time classic "Pudding in a
Cloud."*

2 cups thawed COOL WHIP
   Chocolate Whipped
   Topping
2 cups cold milk
1 package (4-serving size)
   JELL-O Chocolate Flavor
   Instant Pudding and Pie
   Filling

SPOON whipped topping evenly
into 6 dessert dishes. Using back
of spoon, spread whipped topping
into bottom and up sides of each
dish.

POUR milk into large bowl. Add
pudding mix. Beat with wire
whisk 1 to 2 minutes. Let stand
5 minutes or until thickened.
Spoon pudding into dishes.

REFRIGERATE until ready to
serve.   *Makes 6 servings*

Note: Dessert is best made and
served the same day.

*Clockwise from top: Chocolate
Tornado, S'More Squares, Candy
Bar Pie (page 80)*

Double Layer Pumpkin Pie

4 ounces PHILADELPHIA
    BRAND Cream Cheese,
    softened
1 tablespoon milk or
    half-and-half
1 tablespoon sugar
1½ cups thawed COOL WHIP
    Whipped Topping
1 prepared graham cracker
    crumb crust (6 ounces)
1 cup cold milk or
    half-and-half
2 packages (4-serving size)
    JELL-O Vanilla Flavor
    Instant Pudding and Pie
    Filling
1 can (16 ounces) pumpkin
1 teaspoon ground
    cinnamon
½ teaspoon ground ginger
¼ teaspoon ground cloves
    Additional thawed
    COOL WHIP Whipped
    Topping

BEAT cream cheese, 1 tablespoon milk and sugar in large bowl with wire whisk until smooth. Gently stir in whipped topping. Spread on bottom of crust.

POUR 1 cup milk into another large bowl. Add pudding mixes. Beat with wire whisk 1 to 2 minutes. (Mixture will be thick.) Stir in pumpkin and spices with wire whisk until well mixed. Spread over cream cheese layer.

REFRIGERATE 4 hours or until set. Garnish with additional whipped topping. Store leftover pie in refrigerator.

Makes 8 servings

Helpful Tip: Soften cream cheese in microwave on HIGH 15 to 20 seconds.

Cranberry Raspberry Mousse

1 cup cranberry juice
    cocktail
1 package (4-serving size)
    JELL-O Brand Raspberry
    Flavor Gelatin
1 container (12 ounces)
    cranberry raspberry
    crushed fruit
1 tub (12 ounces)
    COOL WHIP Whipped
    Topping, thawed

BRING cranberry juice to boil in small saucepan. Dissolve gelatin completely in boiling liquid in large bowl. Stir in fruit. Refrigerate until slightly thickened.

STIR in 2 cups of the whipped topping until well blended. Layer cranberry mixture and 2 cups of the remaining whipped topping alternately in 8 dessert glasses.

REFRIGERATE 3 hours or until firm. Garnish each dessert with dollop of remaining whipped topping. *Makes 8 servings*

Clockwise from top right: Frosted Spice Cake (page 81), Double Layer Pumpkin Pie, Cranberry Raspberry Mousse

Caramel Apple Squares
Photo on page 69

Creamy COOL WHIP complements the best of the season's apple harvest.

    11 graham cracker squares
    22 KRAFT Caramels
     3 tablespoons milk
    2/3 cup chopped walnuts
     1 cup cold milk
     1 package (4-serving size)
        JELL-O Vanilla Flavor
        Instant Pudding and Pie
        Filling
     2 cups thawed COOL WHIP
        Whipped Topping
     2 cups diced red and/or
        green apples
    1/4 cup KRAFT Miniature
        Marshmallows

ARRANGE crackers in bottom of 12×8-inch baking dish, cutting crackers to fit, if necessary.

MICROWAVE 15 of the caramels and 2 tablespoons of the milk in small microwavable bowl on HIGH 1 to 1 1/2 minutes or until caramels are melted and mixture is smooth, stirring after 1 minute. Spread over crackers; sprinkle with 1/3 cup of the walnuts. Refrigerate.

POUR 1 cup milk into large bowl. Add pudding mix. Beat with wire whisk 1 to 2 minutes. Gently stir in 1 cup of the whipped topping. Spread over caramel layer.

REFRIGERATE at least 3 hours or until ready to serve. Garnish with remaining whipped topping, 1/3 cup walnuts, apples and marshmallows. Microwave remaining 7 caramels and

1 tablespoon milk in small microwavable bowl on HIGH 1 minute or until caramels are melted and mixture is smooth, stirring after 30 seconds. Drizzle over top of dessert. Store leftover dessert in refrigerator.
Makes 10 servings

Apple Crunch: Mix equal amounts of **COOL WHIP LITE Whipped Topping** and plain or vanilla flavored lowfat yogurt. Spoon over diced red and green apples and granola cereal. Sprinkle with ground cinnamon.

Candy Bar Pie
Photo on page 77

     1 pint vanilla ice cream
        (2 cups), softened
     1 prepared chocolate flavor
        crumb crust (6 ounces)
    1/2 cup caramel sauce or
        dessert topping
    1/2 cup chopped peanuts
     1 tub (8 ounces) COOL WHIP
        Chocolate Whipped
        Topping, thawed

SPREAD ice cream evenly in bottom of crust. Freeze until ice cream is firm.

SPREAD caramel sauce over ice cream; sprinkle with peanuts. Cover with whipped topping.

FREEZE 4 hours or until firm. Let stand at room temperature 15 minutes or until pie can be cut easily. Store leftover pie in freezer.
Makes 8 servings

Chocolate Striped Delight

35 chocolate sandwich
    cookies, finely crushed
    (3 cups)
6 tablespoons margarine,
    melted
1 package (8 ounces)
    PHILADELPHIA BRAND
    Cream Cheese, softened
1/4 cup sugar
2 tablespoons milk
1 tub (8 ounces) COOL WHIP
    Chocolate Whipped
    Topping, thawed
3 1/4 cups cold milk
2 packages (4-serving size)
    JELL-O Chocolate Flavor
    Instant Pudding and Pie
    Filling

MIX crushed cookies and margarine in medium bowl. Press firmly into bottom of 13×9-inch pan. Refrigerate 15 minutes.

BEAT cream cheese, sugar and 2 tablespoons milk in medium bowl until smooth. Gently stir in 1 1/4 cups of the whipped topping. Spread over crust.

POUR 3 1/4 cups milk into large bowl. Add pudding mixes. Beat with wire whisk 1 to 2 minutes. Pour over cream cheese layer. Let stand 5 minutes. Drop remaining whipped topping by spoonfuls over pudding. Spread to cover pudding.

REFRIGERATE 4 hours or overnight. Cut into squares.
Makes 18 servings

Helpful Tip: For easier cutting, place dessert in freezer 1 hour before serving.

Frosted Spice Cake
Photo on page 78

This glorious cake will delight your guests with its holiday-spiced flavor.

1 cup cold milk
1 package (4-serving size)
    JELL-O Vanilla Flavor
    Instant Pudding and Pie
    Filling
1 tablespoon grated orange
    peel
1/2 teaspoon ground
    cinnamon
1/4 teaspoon ground nutmeg
1 tub (8 ounces) COOL WHIP
    Whipped Topping,
    thawed
2 baked 9-inch round spice
    or yellow cake layers,
    cooled
Chopped nuts (optional)

POUR milk into large bowl. Add pudding mix, orange peel and spices. Beat with wire whisk 1 to 2 minutes. Gently stir in whipped topping.

FILL and frost cake layers with whipped topping mixture. Pipe additional whipped topping mixture around bottom of cake (see page 7 for directions), if desired. Garnish with chopped nuts. Store cake in refrigerator.
Makes 12 servings

Year-Round Fun for Kids

Looking for fun activities you can do with your child? This chapter features easy-to-follow recipes that are fun to make and delicious to eat. Many are so simple the kids can even help.

Hit a home run with the **Baseball Mitt Cake** and **Cool Cookie-wiches.** Create magic with **Butterfly Cupcakes** and **Doggone Delicious Birthday Dessert** at your child's next party.

Recipes like **Tic-Tac-Toe Pie** and **Clown Cones** will help moms and dads make every day a "funday."

Wild Side Sundaes (page 94)

Tic-Tac-Toe Pie

Play a fast game of tic-tac-toe as you put the finishing touches on this creamy frozen pie.

> **Vanilla wafer cookies**
> 1½ **cups cold milk**
> 1 **package (4-serving size) JELL-O Vanilla Flavor Instant Pudding and Pie Filling**
> 1 **tub (8 ounces) COOL WHIP Whipped Topping, thawed**
> **Assorted miniature cookies**

LINE bottom and sides of 9-inch pie plate with vanilla wafer cookies.

POUR milk into large bowl. Add pudding mix. Beat with wire whisk 1 to 2 minutes. Let stand 5 minutes or until slightly thickened. Gently stir in 3 cups of the whipped topping. Spoon into crust.

FREEZE 4 hours or overnight until firm. Let stand at room temperature 15 minutes or until pie can be cut easily. Garnish with remaining whipped topping to form lines. Decorate with miniature cookies between the lines to resemble a tic-tac-toe game. Store leftover pie in freezer.
Makes 8 servings

Funny Face Cookies

Decorating these funny faces is an activity that includes your children in the fun!

> 4 **large cookies (about 4 inches in diameter)**
> ½ **cup thawed COOL WHIP Whipped Topping or COOL WHIP Chocolate Whipped Topping**
> **Assorted candies and sprinkles**
> **BAKER'S Semi-Sweet Real Chocolate Chips**
> **Toasted BAKER'S ANGEL FLAKE Coconut (see page 9 for directions)**

SPREAD each cookie with about 2 tablespoons of the whipped topping.

DECORATE with candies, sprinkles, chips and coconut to resemble faces. Serve immediately.
Makes 4 servings

Creamy Cookie Parfaits

> 24 **to 32 miniature cookies**
> 2⅔ **cups thawed COOL WHIP Whipped Topping or COOL WHIP Chocolate Whipped Topping**

LAYER cookies and whipped topping alternately in 4 parfait glasses. Top with additional cookies. Serve immediately or refrigerate until ready to serve.
Makes 4 servings

Counter-clockwise from top right: Creamy Cookie Parfaits, Tic-Tac-Toe Pie, Funny Face Cookies

Creamy Carousel Dessert

4 cups cold milk
2 packages (4-serving size) JELL-O Chocolate Flavor Instant Pudding and Pie Filling
1 tub (8 ounces) COOL WHIP Chocolate Whipped Topping, thawed
Multi-colored sprinkles
4 or 5 plastic straws
8 to 10 animal crackers
Paper carousel roof (see directions below)

POUR milk into large bowl. Add pudding mixes. Beat with wire whisk 1 to 2 minutes. Pour into 1½-quart serving bowl. Let stand 5 minutes. Spread whipped topping over pudding.

REFRIGERATE at least 1 hour or until set. Sprinkle with multi-colored sprinkles. Arrange straws and animal crackers on whipped topping as shown in photograph.

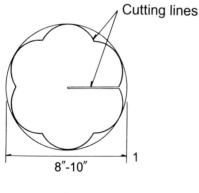

Cutting lines

8"-10"

CUT 8- to 10-inch circle from colored paper; scallop edges, if desired. Make 1 slit to center as shown in illustration 1. Overlap cut edges together to form carousel roof; secure with tape as shown in illustration 2. Place on top of straws. Serve immediately or refrigerate until ready to serve.
Makes 12 servings

Clown Cones

2 cups cold milk
1 package (4-serving size) JELL-O Vanilla or Chocolate Flavor Instant Pudding and Pie Filling
1 tub (8 ounces) COOL WHIP Whipped Topping, thawed
Paper baking cups
12 sugar ice cream cones
Assorted candies and sprinkles
Decorating gel

POUR milk into large bowl. Add pudding mix. Beat with wire whisk 1 to 2 minutes. Let stand 5 minutes. Gently stir in whipped topping. Pour into 2-quart freezer container; cover.

FREEZE 6 hours or overnight until firm. Let stand to soften slightly. Scoop onto flattened baking cups.

TOP with ice cream cones for hats. Make clown faces with candies and decorating gel. Decorate cones as desired. Serve immediately. *Makes 12*

Top to bottom: Creamy Carousel Dessert, Clown Cones

YOU'RE INVITED

Cool Cookie-wiches

1 tub (8 ounces) COOL WHIP
  Whipped Topping,
  thawed
24 cookies
  Multi-colored sprinkles
  Finely crushed chocolate
  cookies

SPREAD whipped topping about
3/4 inch thick on 1 cookie. Place
another cookie lightly on top. Roll
or lightly press edges in sprinkles
or crushed cookies. Repeat with
remaining ingredients.

FREEZE 4 hours or until firm.
Wrap individually and store in
freezer for up to 2 weeks.
Makes 12

Baseball Mitt Cake

1 package (2-layer size) cake
  mix, any flavor except
  angel food
1 1/2 cups thawed COOL WHIP
  Chocolate Whipped
  Topping
1/4 cup chocolate sprinkles
1/2 cup thawed COOL WHIP
  Whipped Topping
  Red string licorice

HEAT oven to 350°F.

PREPARE cake mix as directed on
package. Pour 1/3 cup batter into
greased and floured 6-ounce
custard cup. Divide remaining
batter evenly between 2 greased
and floured 8-inch round cake
pans. Bake 20 minutes for the

custard cup and 35 minutes for
the pans or until toothpick
inserted in centers comes out
clean. Cool 10 minutes; remove
from custard cup and pans. Cool
completely on wire rack. Reserve
1 cake layer for another use.

CUT remaining cake layer as
shown in illustration. Place on
serving plate. Frost with chocolate
whipped topping. Sprinkle with
chocolate sprinkles.

FROST custard cup cake with
white whipped topping. Place on
cake layer as shown in photograph.
Decorate cake with pieces of
licorice as shown in photograph.
Store cake in refrigerator.
Makes 8 servings

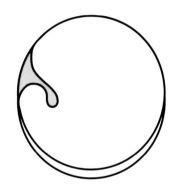

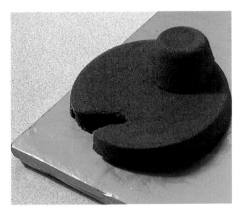

Counter-clockwise from top right:
Electrifying Slide Dessert (page
94), Baseball Mitt Cake, Cool
Cookie-wiches

Doggone Delicious Birthday Dessert

1½ cups cold milk
  1 package (4-serving size)
     JELL-O Chocolate Flavor
     Instant Pudding and Pie
     Filling
  2 tubs (8 ounces) COOL WHIP
     Chocolate Whipped
     Topping, thawed
  3 cups chopped chocolate
     sandwich cookies
  4 chocolate wafer cookies
  2 large black gumdrops
  2 green starlight mints
  2 small green gumdrops
  1 large red gumdrop
    Black or red string licorice
  2 vanilla wafer cookies

LINE 2-quart bowl with plastic wrap.

POUR milk into another large bowl. Add pudding mix. Beat with wire whisk 1 to 2 minutes. Let stand 5 minutes. Gently stir in 1 tub of the whipped topping and chopped cookies. Spoon into prepared bowl; cover.

FREEZE 8 hours or overnight until firm. Invert bowl onto serving plate or tray; remove plastic wrap. Frost with remaining tub whipped topping.

ATTACH chocolate wafer cookies to dessert to form ears. Decorate with candies and pieces of licorice to make dog's face. Place vanilla wafer cookies at base of dessert. Decorate with whipped topping and pieces of licorice to form paws. Let stand at room temperature 10 minutes or until

dessert can be cut easily. Store leftover dessert in freezer.
Makes 10 servings

Butterfly Cupcakes

1 cup cold milk
1 package (4-serving size)
    JELL-O Instant Pudding
    and Pie Filling, any
    flavor
1 tub (8 ounces) COOL WHIP
    Whipped Topping,
    thawed
24 baked cupcakes, cooled
    Multi-colored sprinkles
    Miniature flower candies
    Black or red string licorice

POUR milk into large bowl. Add pudding mix. Beat with wire whisk 1 to 2 minutes. Gently stir in whipped topping. Reserve 1 teaspoon pudding mixture; set aside.

CUT top off each cupcake. Cut each top in half; set aside. Spoon 2 heaping tablespoons pudding mixture on top of each cupcake. Sprinkle with multi-colored sprinkles.

PLACE 2 cupcake top halves, cut sides together, into pudding mixture, raising outside ends slightly to resemble butterfly wings. Lightly dip candies into reserved pudding mixture; arrange on cupcake wings. Insert pieces of licorice into pudding mixture to resemble antennae. Store cupcakes in refrigerator. *Makes 24*

Left to right: Butterfly Cupcakes,
Doggone Delicious Birthday
Dessert

Flowerpot Pie

1 cup cold milk
1 package (4-serving size) JELL-O Chocolate Flavor Instant Pudding and Pie Filling
1 tub (8 ounces) COOL WHIP Whipped Topping, thawed
20 chocolate sandwich cookies, finely crushed
1½ cups "rocks"*
1 prepared chocolate flavor or graham cracker crumb crust (6 ounces)
  Gumdrop Flowers (see directions on this page) (optional)
 *Use any combination of the following:
  BAKER'S Semi-Sweet Real Chocolate Chips
  Chopped peanuts
  Granola

POUR milk into large bowl. Add pudding mix. Beat with wire whisk 1 to 2 minutes. Gently stir in whipped topping.

STIR 1 cup of the crushed cookies and "rocks" into pudding mixture. Spoon into crust. Sprinkle with remaining crushed cookies.

FREEZE 4 hours or until firm. Let stand at room temperature 15 minutes or until pie can be cut easily. Garnish with Gumdrop Flowers. Store leftover pie in freezer.   *Makes 8 servings*

Gumdrop Flowers: Flatten small gumdrops. Cut with small cookie cutters. Attach to pretzel sticks to form flowers and leaves as shown in photograph.

Honey Bees

A hint of honey adds zip to this cute snack.

1 cup cold milk
3 tablespoons honey
  Yellow food coloring (optional)
1 package (4-serving size) JELL-O Vanilla Flavor Instant Pudding and Pie Filling
2 cups thawed COOL WHIP Whipped Topping
¾ cup finely crushed chocolate wafer cookies
12 chocolate wafer cookie halves
6 large black gumdrops
  Black or red string licorice

POUR milk, honey and food coloring into large bowl. Add pudding mix. Beat with wire whisk 1 to 2 minutes.

STIR in whipped topping. Layer alternately with crushed cookies in 6 dessert dishes.

REFRIGERATE 1 hour or until ready to serve. Place cookie halves in whipped topping mixture to form wings. Decorate with gumdrops. Insert small pieces of licorice to form antennae and stinger. Sprinkle with additional crushed cookies, if desired.
          Makes 6 servings

Clockwise from top: Honey Bees, Wormy Apples (page 94), Flowerpot Pie

Wild Side Sundaes
Photo on page 83

**4 packages (4-serving size)
JELL-O Brand Gelatin,
4 different flavors
4 cups boiling water
2 cups cold water
1 tub (8 ounces) COOL WHIP
Whipped Topping,
thawed
Additional thawed
COOL WHIP Whipped
Topping**

DISSOLVE each package of
gelatin completely in 1 cup boiling
water in separate bowls. Stir
1/2 cup cold water into each bowl
of gelatin. Pour each mixture into
separate 8-inch square pans.
Refrigerate at least 3 hours or until
firm. Cut gelatin in each pan into
1/2-inch cubes.

LAYER gelatin cubes alternately
with whipped topping in sundae
glasses. Garnish with dollop of
additional whipped topping.

REFRIGERATE until ready to
serve.   *Makes 16 servings*

Electrifying Slide Dessert
Photo on page 88

**2 packages (4-serving size)
JELL-O Brand Gelatin,
any flavor
2 cups boiling water
1 cup cold water
Ice cubes
2 cups thawed COOL WHIP
Whipped Topping**

LINE bottom and sides of 2 loaf
pans with wet paper towels. Tilt
3 (8-ounce) glasses in each loaf pan.

DISSOLVE 1 package of the
gelatin completely in 1 cup boiling
water in large bowl. Mix 1/2 cup
cold water and ice to make 1 cup.
Add to gelatin, stirring until ice is
melted. Refrigerate 10 minutes or
until slightly thickened. Gently
stir in 1 cup of the whipped
topping. Spoon into tilted glasses.
Refrigerate 1 hour or until set but
not firm.

DISSOLVE remaining package
gelatin completely in 1 cup boiling
water in medium bowl. Mix
1/2 cup cold water and ice to make
1 cup. Add to gelatin, stirring until
ice is melted. Refrigerate about
10 minutes or until slightly
thickened. Spoon into glasses over
set gelatin mixture. Set glasses
upright.

REFRIGERATE at least 1 hour or
until firm. Garnish with dollop of
remaining whipped topping.
            Makes 6 servings

Wormy Apples
Photo on page 92

**2 small apples
1/2 cup thawed COOL WHIP
Whipped Topping
2 gummy worms**

CORE apples, if desired. Cut each
apple horizontally into 3 slices.

SPREAD slices with whipped
topping. Reassemble apples. Cut
small holes in apples; insert
gummy worms into holes. Serve
immediately.   *Makes 2 servings*

Index

A

Apple Desserts
 Apple Crunch, 80
 Caramel Apple Salad, 48
 Caramel Apple Squares, 80

B

Baby Booties, 43
Baseball Mitt Cake, 89
Berries Delight, 45
Berry Shortcake Shortcuts, 46
Black Forest Torte, 31
Boo the Ghost, 72
Boston Cream Croissants, 48
Butterfly Cupcakes, 90

C

Cakes (*see also* **Shortcakes; Tortes**)
 Baby Booties, 43
 Baseball Mitt Cake, 89
 Boo the Ghost, 72
 Butterfly Cupcakes, 90
 Candy Box Heart, 28
 Candy Cane Cake, 16
 Creamy Orange Cake, 62
 Easter Bonnet Cake, 36
 Firecrackers, 54
 Football Cut-Up Cake, 24
 Frosted Spice Cake, 81
 Hippity Hop Bunny Cake, 39
 Ice Cream Cone Cakes, 72
 Snowballs, 27
Candy Bar Pie, 80
Candy Box Heart, 28
Candy Cane Cake, 16
Cannoli Parfaits, 36
Caramel Apple Salad, 48
Caramel Apple Squares, 80
Cherries Jubilee, 31
Chocolate Banana Berry Trifle, 66
Chocolate Caramel Parfaits, 66
Chocolate Cookie Parfaits, 75
Chocolate Mousse, 32
Chocolate Peanut Butter Desserts, 23
Chocolate Peanut Butter Truffles, 19
Chocolate Peppermint Pie, 16
Chocolate Strawberry Hearts, 28
Chocolate Striped Delight, 81
Chocolate Tornado, 76
Chocolate Truffle Loaf, 44

Christmas Ornament Dessert, 19
Classic Ambrosia, 41
Clown Cones, 86
Cookies and Cream Pie, 67
Cool Christmas Fudge, 19
Cool Cookie-wiches, 89
Cranberry Raspberry Mousse, 79
Crazy Colored Halloween Desserts, 75
Creamy Carousel Dessert, 86
Creamy Cookie Parfaits, 85
Creamy Lemon Bars, 45
Creamy Orange Cake, 62
Crumb crusts, 8
Cupcakes (*see* **Cakes**)
Cup of Chocolate Dessert, 27

D

Dessert Grillers, 57
Dessert Nachos, 24
Dessert Pizza, 61
Dessert Waffles, 43
Doggone Delicious Birthday
 Dessert, 90
Double Layer Pumpkin Pie, 79

E

Easter Bonnet Cake, 36
Eggnog Trifle, 20
Electrifying Slide Dessert, 94

F

Father's Day Cheesecake Pie, 57
Firecrackers, 54
Flowerpot Pie, 93
Football Cut-Up Cake, 24
4th of July Dessert, 54
Frosted Spice Cake, 81
Frozen Strawberry-Yogurt Pie, 67
Funny Face Cookies, 85

G

German Sweet Chocolate Pie, 17
Gumdrop Flowers: 13, 93

H

Heavenly Ambrosia in a Cloud, 41
Hippity Hop Bunny Cake, 39
Honey Bees, 93

I

Ice Cream Cone Cakes, 72

L

Lemonade Stand Pie, 65
Lemon Berry Charlotte, 41
Lemon Berry Terrine, 58
Lemon Cheese Squares, 62
Lemon Chiffon Pie, 45

M

Mandarin Mirror, 20
Merry Berry Desserts, 17
Mini Ladyfinger Napoleons, 23
Mint Chocolate Cookie Parfaits, 75
Monkey Bars, 71
Mousses
    Chocolate Mousse, 32
    Cranberry Raspberry Mousse, 79

P

Parfaits
    Cannoli Parfaits, 36
    Cherries Jubilee, 31
    Chocolate Caramel Parfaits, 66
    Chocolate Cookie Parfaits, 75
    Chocolate Peanut Butter Desserts, 23
    Creamy Cookie Parfaits, 85
    Mint Chocolate Cookie Parfaits, 75
    St. Patrick's Parfaits, 32
Peaches and Cream Dessert, 23
Peanut Pockets, 71
Pies, Frozen
    Candy Bar Pie, 80
    Cookies and Cream Pie, 67
    Flowerpot Pie, 93
    Frozen Strawberry-Yogurt Pie, 67
    German Sweet Chocolate Pie, 17
    Lemonade Stand Pie, 65
    Strawberry Banana Split Pie, 61
    Tic-Tac-Toe Pie, 85
Pies, Refrigerated
    Chocolate Peppermint Pie, 16
    Double Layer Pumpkin Pie, 79
    Father's Day Cheesecake Pie, 57
    Lemon Chiffon Pie, 45
    Romanoff Tarts, 58
    Strawberry Cool 'n Easy Pie, 45
    Summer Lime Pie, 65
Pistachio Pineapple Delight, 67

R

Rainbow Sandwiches, 75
Raspberry Shortcake, 46

Raspberry Vanilla Pudding Supreme, 44
Romanoff Tarts, 58

S

Shortcakes
    Berry Shortcake Shortcuts, 46
    Chocolate Strawberry Hearts, 28
    Raspberry Shortcake, 46
    Shortcake Dessert, 46
    "Shortcake" in a Cloud, 46
    Traditional Shortcake, 46
S'More Squares, 76
Snacks
    Chocolate Tornado, 76
    Clown Cones, 86
    Cool Cookie-wiches, 89
    Crazy Colored Halloween Desserts, 75
    Dessert Nachos, 24
    Electrifying Slide Dessert, 94
    Funny Face Cookies, 85
    Honey Bees, 93
    Mini Ladyfinger Napoleons, 23
    Monkey Bars, 71
    Peanut Pockets, 71
    Rainbow Sandwiches, 75
    S'More Squares, 76
    Star Spangled Snack, 54
    Wild Side Sundaes, 94
    Wormy Apples, 94
Snowballs, 27
Stars and Stripes Dessert, 53
Star Spangled Snack, 54
St. Patrick's Parfaits, 32
Strawberry Angel Torte, 46
Strawberry Banana Split Pie, 61
Strawberry Cool 'n Easy Pie, 45
Strawberry Dip, 48
Strawberry Heart Pillows, 66
Summer Lime Pie, 65

T

Tic-Tac-Toe Pie, 85
Tortes
    Black Forest Torte, 31
    Strawberry Angel Torte, 46
Traditional Shortcake, 46
Trifles
    Chocolate Banana Berry Trifle, 66
    Eggnog Trifle, 20
    Peaches and Cream Dessert, 23
Tropical Expressions, 27

W

Watermelon Slices, 53
Wild Side Sundaes, 94
Wormy Apples, 94